BASICS OF BUDGETING

Basics of Budgeting

Robert G. Finney

A Sue Katz & Associates Book

amacom

American Management Association

New York • Atlanta • Boston • Chicago • Kansas City • San Francisco • Washington, D.C.
Brussels • Toronto • Mexico City • Tokyo

*This book is available at a special
discount when ordered in bulk quantities.
For information, contact Special Sales Department,
AMACOM, a division of American Management Association,
135 West 50th Street, New York, NY 10020.*

This publication is designed to provide accurate and authoritative information in regard to the subject matter covered. It is sold with the understanding that the publisher is not engaged in rendering legal, accounting, or other professional service. If legal advice or other expert assistance is required, the services of a competent professional person should be sought.

Library of Congress Cataloging-in-Publication Data

*Finney, Robert G.
    Basics of budgeting / Robert G. Finney.
        p.   cm.
    "A Sue Katz and Associates book."
    Includes bibliographical references and index.
    ISBN 0-8144-7822-0
    1. Budget in business.   I. Title.
HG4028.B8F558   1994
658.15'4—dc20   93-29948
                                              CIP*

© *1994 Robert G. Finney
A Sue Katz & Associates Book
All rights reserved.
Printed in the United States of America.*

*This publication may not be reproduced,
stored in a retrieval system,
or transmitted in whole or in part,
in any form or by any means, electronic,
mechanical, photocopying, recording, or otherwise,
without the prior written permission of AMACOM,
a division of American Management Association,
135 West 50th Street, New York, NY 10020.*

Printing number

10   9   8   7   6   5   4   3   2   1

Contents

Introduction		1
Part I.	**The Nature of Budgeting**	**3**
1.	The Scope of Budgeting for Managers	5
2.	What to Expect at Budget Time	9
3.	Why Is Budgeting So Difficult?	21
Part II.	**The Planning Work of Budgeting**	**29**
4.	Planning	31
5.	Defining the Organization's Work	45
6.	Understanding Costs and Cost Drivers	55
7.	Dealing With Uncertainty: Assumptions	67
8.	Improving Performance: Gap Analysis	77
Part III.	**Generating the Numbers**	**89**
9.	Proper Budget Content	91
10.	Revenue Forecasting	101
11.	Cost Estimating	113
12.	Capital Budgeting	125
Part IV.	**Putting It Together and Selling It**	**139**
13.	A Manager's Budgeting Process	141
14.	Getting the Budget Approved	151

Appendix A.	The Language of Accounting	159
Appendix B.	Glossary of Accounting Terms Used in Budgeting	173
Appendix C.	Use of Personal Computers in Budgeting	181
Bibliography		191
Index		195

BASICS OF BUDGETING

Introduction

Budgeting is often a daunting activity, approached in some companies with a strange mixture of disinterest and awe. "We only have a week to do this, so throw something together so we can get back to interesting work. But, by the way, you will not be allowed to exceed the costs in your budget next year, no matter what happens." There are many anxieties associated with budgeting: It starts too early to predict the next year, it is done under extreme time pressure, and continuous improvement is expected in organization performance.

Managers often perceive budgeting as an irrational "game" whose rules have never been explained to them. Managers work hard at budgeting, but hardly any of them, from the president down to the lowest-level manager, are satisfied with their results.

It need not be this way. Budgeting has the potential for being a manager's most valuable planning and management tool. In these days of heavy competition on all fronts, companies and their managers need all the tools possible if they are going to succeed. They cannot afford to let their budgeting tool remain so dull and rusty.

Budgeting is a management problem, not an accounting problem—a planning activity, not a computational exercise. It is not mysterious and does not require some special sort of logic. It requires mainly the talents that most managers have demonstrated to get their jobs in the first place: planning, forecasting, estimating, and selling. It also requires, in common with any business activity, knowledge of a body of pertinent principles, approaches, and techniques.

This book will sharpen that budgeting tool, providing business managers with the information they need to complete successful budgets. "Successful budgets" are those that will be approved, will authorize the needed resources, give managers maximum value toward job performance and satisfaction, and protect them from irrationality and surprises.

The Importance of Budgeting

Budgeting is a necessary activity and one that is required of most managers. Managers live and work in the future as well as the present. Planning is a major element of any management job. A budget is the numerical expression of the plans for the next year. Because it is specific and immediate, it is an important management tool.

From a positive point of view, the budget is the *only* instrument that can give reality to objectives, strategies, priorities, and plans. Whatever you want to accomplish, it cannot be done unless resources have been provided for that accomplishment. Similarly, goals take on meaning when reflected in the budget and have no meaning when not so reflected.

From a negative point of view, the budget will be used to control managers' activities, and their performances will be measured against their budgets. Poor budgeting hurts credibility, an important asset for any manager. Anytime a manager gets approval to do anything, it is partly an expression of faith by higher management. An important element of that faith is the manager's track record—has he or she done what was promised in the past? Poor budgeting is a fast way to hurt your chances of getting your future favorite ideas approved.

As managers approach a new year, they know that it will present unexpected problems. While the known problems are usually bad enough, they will probably be blindsided by some unpleasant surprises. The best weapons a manager can have for a hostile new year are good plans and forecasts, with the approval of superiors who fully understand them—that is, good budgets.

Part I
The Nature of Budgeting

1
The Scope of Budgeting for Managers

What managers most need from budgeting is approval of the resources needed to accomplish the work required of their organizations. We need not be concerned (except to provide context) with budgeting theories or what the board of directors or the controller will do with the budget. Beyond what we need for budgeting, neither do we need to become experts in related subjects like accounting and investment analysis. The manager's problem is that budget forms have just arrived on his or her desk, and he or she must *do something*. Our concern is thus the manager's work of budgeting.

The general flow of budgeting work is shown in Figure 1-1. Developing organization budgets and relating them to other organizations is the subject of this book. The company budget is further detailed in Figure 2-1 in Chapter 2. The process of planning the work is expanded in Figure 4-5 in Chapter 4, that of generating the numbers in Figure 9-1 in Chapter 9.

The Manager's Work of Budgeting

The manager's work of budgeting is threefold (see Figure 1-2). First, managers must plan their organizations' work for next year. The planning work of budgeting is the subject of Part II. Chapters 4 through 6 treat the subjects that must be understood to plan an organization's work: how to plan, the best way to define an organization's work, what

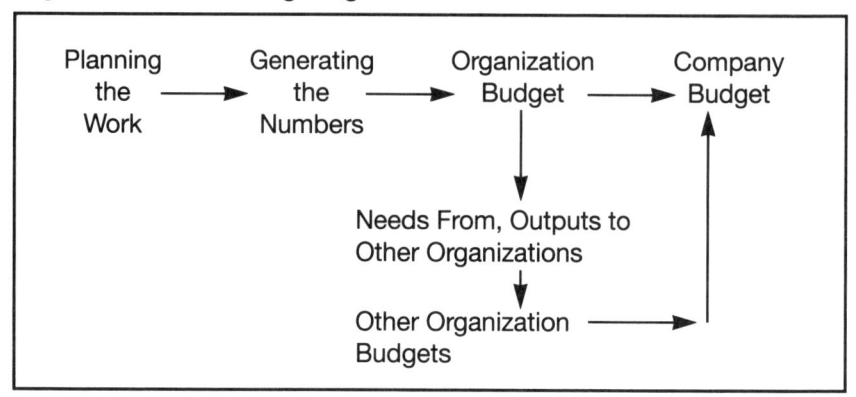

Figure 1-1. The budgeting work flow.

```
Planning  ──►  Generating  ──►  Organization  ──►  Company
  the             the              Budget            Budget
  Work           Numbers              │                ▲
                                      ▼                │
                              Needs From, Outputs to   │
                              Other Organizations      │
                                      │                │
                                      ▼                │
                              Other Organization ──────┘
                              Budgets
```

kinds of costs are incurred by a business, and what things drive or determine those costs.

A major issue in the planning work is the treatment of the inherent uncertainty of the future and the uncontrollability of important outside factors that determine performance. Therefore, Chapter 7 is devoted to the assumptions process, the best way to deal with this ever present uncertainty and uncontrollability. Finally, every manager has an obligation to plan continuous organization performance improvement; an excellent tool for accomplishing this is gap analysis, the subject of Chapter 8.

Second, managers must generate the numbers in the budget. In reality, of course, the work of generating the budget numbers is not divorced from the planning work of budgeting. Indeed, predicting numbers is the result, and the natural last step, of the planning. However, it is appropriate to discuss number generation separately, because there is a right way, and a number of wrong ways, to choose the numbers to put into the budget. All the planning work goes for nought if the resulting numbers are predicted poorly. Part III covers proper sources of numerical estimates in general, and then the three major types of numerical forecasts: revenue, costs, and capital.

Third, managers must sell their budgets, obtaining approval of budgets that give them the resources they need for next year to provide their committed outputs. Obviously, developing good budgets is of no benefit if managers cannot sell those good budgets to their bosses. This third necessary element of budgeting work is the subject of Chapter 14.

Organization budgets are not done in a vacuum. An important requirement and a major benefit of good budgeting is the communica-

The Scope of Budgeting for Managers

Figure 1-2. The manager's work of budgeting.

> Planning the Work
>
> Generating the Numbers
>
> Selling the Budget

tion among the different organizations within the company. Each organization must communicate its needs from other organizations and its outputs to other organizations as part of its budget, and this is discussed throughout the book.

Tips and Traps

- Every business is different, and all managers' "particular" budgeting problems are different. However, a large body of principles, techniques, and practices can be applied beneficially to every business. This book will cover these general principles, techniques, and practices—i.e., the *science* of budgeting.

  Managers must learn their own "particulars"—the *art* of budgeting—for themselves. It is not fruitful, for example, to learn generalized types of budget forms, because no two companies' forms are exactly alike. Rather, this book explains the kinds of information needed in budgets, with examples, and urges you to learn your own budget forms thoroughly.

2
What to Expect at Budget Time

A company's budget is the prediction of the financial results of its plans for the coming year.

Top management and the board of directors want a budget because they want a prediction of how much business the company can expect to do, how much that will cost, and what the nature of the costs will be. They want this because the company represents an investment for which they are responsible. They naturally want to know how much profit and cash flow they can expect from that investment. More important, they must decide what the company should do differently to increase profits and cash flow, and therefore, what strategies should be chosen and what actions should be undertaken.

Theoretically, top management could make this prediction by itself, but in a business of any size, this makes no sense. Managers have been appointed to direct and be responsible for all the activities required by the company to conduct its business. Both because of their greater knowledge of the particular activities and because of their responsibility for them, all managers are expected to contribute to the plans and predictions for the next year.

For all these individual managers, the budgeting process proceeds from the lowest-level managers up through each level of the organization. At each level, there are consolidations, reviews, arguments, modifications, and reworked numbers. Each review can change the budgets of all lower levels. The final review by the board of directors can change the budget of every single organization in the company.

This complexity is unavoidable. The activities of any business are inherently complex, requiring a variety of skills, extensive organization, and extensive interaction to carry them out.

The Company Budget

The company budget is really a collection of budgets that predicts its important financial results: orders, sales, profit and loss (P&L), cash flow, and balance sheet. The logical flow of these different budgets is shown in Figure 2-1.

The company budget is built as a consolidation of budgets that match the company's organization structure. For example, consider a midsize product company with a functional organization reporting to the president.

Company

Marketing
Sales
Engineering
Manufacturing
Finance
Human resources

Each of these major departments, of course, has an organization structure within it; for simplicity, we will detail only the sales department (assuming only domestic sales and a geographical sales organization).

Figure 2-1. The company budget.

```
Orders ──────▶ Sales ──────▶ Expense
                 │  ◀────▶      │
                 ▼              ▼
                P&L           Capital
                 │              │
                 ▼              ▼
            Balance Sheet and Cash Flow
```

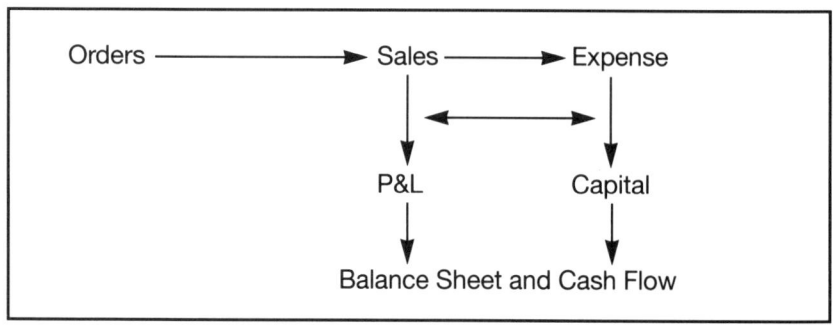

Sales
    Eastern Region Sales
        New England Branch
        Mid-Atlantic Branch
        Southeastern Branch
    Central Region Sales
        Northern Branch
        Southern Branch
        Midwestern Branch
    Western Region Sales
        Southwestern Branch
        Northwestern Branch
        Rocky Mountain Branch
    Sales Administration

Within the sales department, the first budgets generated are those for each of the branches. All the Eastern Region branch budgets are then consolidated into the Eastern Region budget. The budgets of the three regions plus sales administration are then consolidated into the sales department budget. At the same time, the budgets of the other departments are built, level by level, in the same way. Finally, the company budget is the consolidation of all the department budgets.

The budget at each level is the summation of all the budgets at the next lower level, plus the costs and other budget items associated with the manager at that level. There is summarization of information at each level upward. Company budgets are ultimately expressed in accounting and financial reporting terms, but the budgets used by management are in a format that presents the information desired to manage the business. At the lower levels the proper output concerns are units, transactions, and the like, while at higher levels they are dollars of revenue and cash flow.

The Manager's Budget

The budget of each manager fits in the appropriate place in the budget hierarchy that matches the organization. A manager's budget typically contains three types of information:

1. Costs
2. Outputs
3. Supplemental information

Matching the company budget, the information must be supplied for each month of the year.

The way the cost numbers are presented varies from company to company, and function to function. In some cases, managers are asked to present nonfinancial descriptions—man-hours of effort for each project, units of particular items purchased, etc.—that the financial people will then convert into dollars. In other cases, managers themselves will be expected to compute and submit the dollar costs. Costs that represent capital expenditures are submitted separately as part of the capital budget, as discussed in Chapter 12.

The prediction of outputs in the budget is usually not required for all functions but only for those that have financially related and measurable outputs. No organization has outputs more important than payroll: correct payroll checks, delivered on time to each employee. However, the number of paychecks has no direct bearing on company financial results, and the paycheck dollars are accumulated by the organizations in which the employees reside. Thus, while important, payroll outputs are not of direct interest to the budget, and the payroll manager's budget forms will probably not ask for them. (However, all managers should submit their planned outputs as voluntary supplemental information, as discussed in Chapter 5.)

On the other hand, the outputs of factory assembly—the number of units of different types of products delivered to the test function—have a direct bearing on company sales. Assembly managers will undoubtedly be expected to predict the number of units of each type of product or assembly that their organizations will produce during each month of the year. Examples of other organizational outputs for which budget detailing is ordinarily required are shipments, service calls (where they are the basis for revenue), transactions (ditto), collections received, payments made, mortgages closed, insurance policies written, and orders of all kinds received.

Supplemental information may be required with the manager's budget. This requirement can vary widely, but general types are information that helps:

- Explain the budget (e.g., the number of cold calls per period planned by a sales function)
- Evaluate the budget (e.g., results for the three previous years)
- Coordinate different budgets (e.g., requirements for reproductions services)
- Evaluate status versus other goals and problems (e.g., number of minority persons to be hired)

Assumptions are another type of supplemental information requested. Assumptions are always involved, implicitly or explicitly, in developing a budget, because information about the future is always imperfect. If they are not requested, they still should be submitted as voluntary supplemental information. (Assumptions are both a major issue and a powerful tool in every manager's budget. The subject is treated in Chapter 7.)

Budget Forms

Budget forms for a given function and similar types of businesses always call for the same general kinds of information. The differences among companies appear in terminology, the way a particular company is managed and controlled, and the visibility into particulars that different top managements want. The payroll budget form shown in Figure 2-2 is about as simple as a budget form can be.

Total cost is the sum of total salaries, fringe benefits, and total other indirect costs. No delineation of output is requested, because payroll is a function whose outputs do not affect the budget. Labor costs are just salaries, readily identified and tracked by individual names. If new hires were anticipated they would be identified as "New" with an expected salary. Fringe benefits are calculated by a formula included with the budget instructions, most likely a function of salaries and numbers of people. The number and type of "other indirect" cost lines is determined by management's decision concerning the desired visibility of different kinds of costs; indirect costs are often summarized successively in higher-level budgets. Every budget will have an "other" category for indirect costs not itemized.

The budget of a factory assembly function is more extensive. The assembly manager is asked for assembly units (i.e., its outputs), direct labor man-hours, indirect or direct costs in man-hours, indirect labor (dollars), and other indirect costs. (The accounting terms mentioned in this section are defined in Appendix A and in the glossary of accounting terms, Appendix B.) "Assembly units" are divided into projects, and into different elements for each project. Supplemental information includes such things as direct and indirect head count, machine usage in hours, new hires, and layoffs.

A store manager in a chain probably has to budget P&L and cash flow, not just expense. The P&L includes sales (probably by product category), expense (such as salaries, fringe benefits, advertising, rent, utilities, depreciation, outside services, and other), a corporate alloca-

Figure 2-2. Example of a payroll budget form.

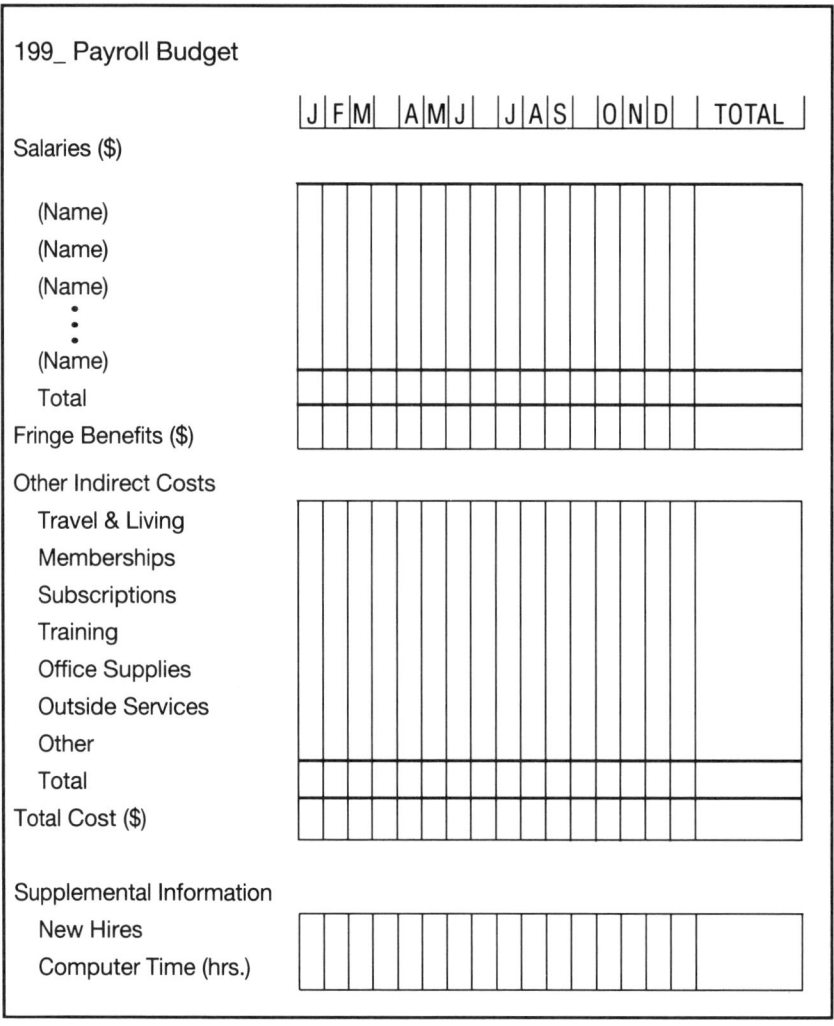

```
199_ Payroll Budget
                          |J|F|M| |A|M|J| |J|A|S| |O|N|D| | TOTAL |
Salaries ($)

  (Name)
  (Name)
  (Name)
    ⋮
  (Name)
  Total
Fringe Benefits ($)

Other Indirect Costs
  Travel & Living
  Memberships
  Subscriptions
  Training
  Office Supplies
  Outside Services
  Other
  Total
Total Cost ($)

Supplemental Information
  New Hires
  Computer Time (hrs.)
```

* Letters in top row stand for months.

tion, and profit before tax. The cash flow budget is in terms of beginning cash, receipts (by product category), disbursements (for inventory by product category and expenses), and ending cash for each month. The store manager also probably has to budget balance sheet items for which he or she is responsible, such as inventory and accounts payable.

Higher-level budget forms reflect different terminology. The manufacturing vice-president's budget, for example, probably includes revenue, cost of goods sold, gross margin (all by project or product), an overhead schedule, and an inventory schedule, as well as summaries of units assembled and shipped and associated direct costs. Other industries have their own parameters of principal interest; in utilities, for example, much of the engineering burdened labor cost goes into a "plant under construction" capital account, and the capital budget form is the most important and extensive one for the utility's engineering vice-president.

Company Prebudgeting Activity

Managers are fortunate if they work for ENLIGHTENED, INC., which has a good budgeting process. Those who work for MUDDLED, INC., are not so fortunate.

Top managers at ENLIGHTENED view the budget as a major planning and management tool and aim to get maximum value from it. They work hard to ensure that the company "thinks it through" before "crunching the numbers." Their budgeting process takes many months, but no numbers are generated until near the end, and iterations and modifications are minimized. ENLIGHTENED top managers see their role as firmly specifying "what," in terms of goals, strategies, priorities, and problems for concentrated attention. They rely upon the rest of the managers, those with the detailed knowledge and information, to decide "how" to carry out their wishes, and "how much" it will cost and use critical resources. Therefore, in preparation for actual budgeting, ENLIGHTENED top managers actively direct:

- Strategic planning
- The identification of outside factors over which the company has no control but that are important determinants of results
- Identification of critical factors for success, problems, and improvements upon which concentration is desired
- Preliminary budget targets that will constitute satisfactory performance

All the managers at ENLIGHTENED, INC., begin their budgets with good knowledge of what the company wants to do next year, what is generally expected of them, and what top management's "hot buttons" are.

The managers at MUDDLED learn that the budgeting process has begun when forms arrive at their desks. The forms are accompanied by a letter from the budget analyst giving a few ground rules (such as "assume salary increases averaging 5 percent") and state that numbers are due back to the analyst in a week or two. There is also a "pep talk" letter from the controller noting the importance of minimizing costs next year. Managers at MUDDLED must invoke all their creativity to complete their budgets.

Your company is probably somewhere between ENLIGHTENED and MUDDLED; let's hope it is closer to the former. (We will refer to ENLIGHTENED, INC. and MUDDLED, INC. from time to time throughout the book.)

The Budgeting Process

Although each contains complexity and hard work, the budgeting process can be described as the five simple steps listed in Figure 2-3.

Concerning the first step in the process, we have already discussed the types of information required from all managers: costs or efforts and unit purchases leading to costs, possibly outputs, and various kinds of supplemental information. At MUDDLED, budget forms are pieces of paper, while at ENLIGHTENED they are diskettes formatted for personal-computer use.

The instructions contain the detailed schedule for the whole company budgeting process, culminating with presentation to the board of directors. They should contain assumptions that are to be made

Figure 2-3. The budgeting process.

---

1. Budget forms and instructions are distributed to all managers.

2. The budget forms are filled out and submitted.

3. The individual budgets are transformed into appropriate budgeting/accounting terms and consolidated into one overall company budget.

4. The budget is reviewed, modified as necessary, and approved.

5. The final budget is then used throughout the year to control and measure the organization.

throughout the company, division, or department. At ENLIGHTENED, they also include a list of uncontrollable items about which the manager should make assumptions, and direct the manager to expand that list when appropriate. General guidance for budget preparation is given, and any changes in procedures or budget format from the previous year are explained.

The completion and submission of budget forms is the manager's activity of actually preparing the budget. The work of planning and generating the numbers that goes into this is the subject of the entire Parts II and III.

At MUDDLED, the manager completes the paper budget form by hand and gives it to the budget analyst, who then manipulates it by hand. At ENLIGHTENED, some managers enter the numbers into the formatted budget diskette on their personal computers and return the completed diskette to the budget analyst. Other managers have personal computers that are part of a network; they enter the budget numbers into the network, to be accessed electronically by the budget analyst. The ENLIGHTENED budget analysts then do their manipulation automatically, eliminating a large source of budget errors and inconsistencies.

The transformation and consolidation of the budgets is done by accounting, by the people we call "budget analysts." (They may have different titles, but every company has one or more people who are responsible for collecting, manipulating, and integrating budgets, checking them for consistency and accuracy, and administering the budgeting process.) Budget numbers such as units and man-hours are translated into dollars. Allocated costs (e.g., facility expense) are added into the manager's budget. Burden rates are computed and factored in when and as appropriate. This part of the process is interleaved with the next step—review, modification, and approval. Together, they are a step-by-step, repetitive progression up the levels of the organization. As the process of consolidation moves up the organization, the terms of accumulation change from the specific-activity format at the lower levels toward the financial statements format used for the overall company.

The first review is by the manager's boss. The manager's budget will have been translated into dollars but is probably still in the specific-activity format. All the budgets for the boss's organization will have been consolidated to give the boss a first look at his or her overall budget. In this review the manager is expected to explain, justify, and defend the submitted numbers. With the help of the budget analyst, there are comparisons with the budgets of interacting organizations to check consistency.

When the boss has approved all subordinate budgets, the process is repeated at the next level. The boss's budget is transformed and consolidated with peer organizations to provide the budget for the manager at the next-higher level. That manager than reviews the budgets for all his or her subordinates, and so on.

Each review might cause changes, which then have to be reflected back down the organization. This process can take months, and be full of surprises for all managers. They might believe, more than once, that their budgets have been approved, only to find expenses cut and/or outputs increased *again* as a result of higher management review.

This iterative process ends with final review (which might result in yet another round of changes) and approval of the total company budget by the board of directors. This board review is typically held at the last board meeting before the new (budget) year begins. After board approval, the final budgets are distributed to all managers.

The final step, use of the budget for control and measurement, continues throughout the budget year. The final budget is the manager's "bible." There will be at least a monthly review of results versus budget, and sometimes reference to it almost daily. Every change that comes up, and everything the manager wants to do, will be considered against the numbers in the budget. If the manager's budget is being met, he or she can expect relative peace. If the numbers are being missed, he or she should expect to have to explain and defend the variations, and to be required to develop corrective action. Managers may propose changes in work and costs that are logical in the light of changed conditions; however, if such changes violate the budget, their approval may be difficult to obtain.

In other words, after all the hard work, time pressure, and changes in the environment and in the budget, the resulting document tends to be "cast in concrete" and hung firmly around your neck. It can get heavy as the year goes on. But this is the kind of pressure you signed up for when you wanted to become a manager. What you have to do is find ways to lighten the load, and that is what we will address.

Why Annual Budgets?

Businesses tend to have natural predictive cycles, and few of these tend to be just one year. A company whose business is large, long-term construction contracts might be able to predict its business well for two or three years. Companies that rely on a small number of large orders, such as a manufacturer of large computers, may not be able to predict their businesses confidently more than six months ahead. Businesses that make a large number of small sales, such as most retail businesses, must base predictions on the pertinent market, competition, and economy. These things change slowly for some businesses, rapidly for others.

So why not pick a natural predictive cycle for the budget? Why must there be an annual budget when it does not fit the predictive cycle? The answer is that the investment and lending communities keep score based on annual periods (and, to a lesser extent, on quarters of a year). Public companies are required to report financial results annually and quarterly. Investors and lenders measure the company on the basis of these reports. Since the budget is both the plan and the scorecard, it must focus on those same annual and quarterly time periods.

Theoretically, a privately owned company could choose a different budget period. However, if it ever needs to borrow money or wishes to compare itself to competitors, or to the world of business and finance in general, it must structure its numbers in the same annual and quarterly increments that are used by that world.

Therefore, with only rare exceptions, the word "budget" means "annual budget" in business. We will always assume that budgets are for one year.

These annual budgets are often fleshed out with plans for particular periods and activities during the year such as quarterly plans, plans for a peak season like Christmas, or "budgets" for individual television productions. These represent necessary and desirable detailed planning and prediction, within the framework of the primary annual budget.

The year for which the budget is prepared is the company's "fiscal year." The fiscal year for a business is the twelve-month period for which financial results and statements are prepared and reported. Companies are allowed to choose their fiscal year, and, for good reasons, many use a fiscal year that differs from the calendar year. Companies that have high Christmas peaks of business, for example, might move the fiscal year away from the calendar year so the extensive year-end accounting work can be done at a time that is not so busy. For simplicity of discussion, we always implicitly assume that the fiscal year equals the calendar year.

Tips and Traps

- Even if a casual approach is taken to the budget in your company, it is a mistake to assume that the company believes the budget is unimportant. In some companies there is an absolute prohibition against overspending a budget. In most companies a missed budget will be taken seriously, always resulting in pressure, often requiring corrective action. Even if the budget is truly not important, managers who miss budgets are handy whipping boys and girls if profit problems surface during the year.

- If you are given paper budget forms rather than a diskette, take the time to program your forms into a spreadsheet on your personal computer. (See Appendix C, Use of Personal Computers in Budgeting.) This will pay off in ease of manipulation and changes, as well as in investigating various alternatives.

3

Why Is Budgeting So Difficult?

Difficulties with budgeting are not primarily caused by stupidity; a company populated with only the best and brightest of people would still have budgeting problems. There are inherent problems in budgeting that are fundamental to any budgeting situation (see Figure 3-1).

Of course, MUDDLED, INC., has plenty of man-made problems associated with its budgets. The numbers are generated so early that they are often out of date before the budget year begins. Preparation and top management guidance are minimal, and managers are under extreme time pressure at every step. Reviews tend to be long and emotional "can so, cannot" sessions. However, even ENLIGHTENED, INC., has problems preparing good budgets.

These fundamental problems will not go away. They must be understood and addressed for budgeting to have value. The five inherent problems of budgeting will be described in this chapter. All these problems are related and reinforce each other.

The Conflict of Objectives

There are a number of valid objectives of the budgeting process, and they differ from participant to participant. The good news is that these differing objectives are generally compatible. The bad news is that every manager has two objectives that are contradictory, and this conflict is budgeting's first inherent problem.

Consider the objectives of different people involved with budgets.

Figure 3-1. The inherent problems of budgeting.

> The Conflict of Objectives
>
> Measurement
>
> The Uncertainty of the Future
>
> The Uncontrollability of the Outside Environment
>
> The Psychological Nature of Budgeting

The Owner's Objectives

The owner or owners of a business want a budget that plans the best profit realistically achievable. The owner also wants the budget to be accurate and consistent with the chosen strategy. If the owner wants to do business only in the United States, he or she does not want dollars in the budget for international sales effort. Owners also want their companies to be well managed, and so want the budget to contain the information most useful to management and to communicate strategy and plans across the whole organization. Finally, owners want a budget that facilitates goal setting and measurement.

The President's Objectives

The president generally wants the same things as the owners, but also wants a budget that will be beaten. The president's power and job security are usually heavily based upon his or her credibility, and protecting that credibility is important. His or her incentive compensation will probably also be based, at least in part, on performance versus budget. Thus the last thing a president wants is a budget that promises the moon when a low earth orbit is all that can be achieved.

The Managers' Objectives

When we come to managers, their main concerns are knowing what their organizations are expected to accomplish, and having enough resources to carry out their responsibilities. Their primary budgeting objectives are to understand their required outputs, what resources they will have, how they will interface with other organizations, and what support they will get. They also share the owners' and president's objectives: They want to work for a profitable, healthy company, they want to know the strategy and to have the most useful information, etc. All managers have the obligation to improve performance and to achieve the best results possible under given conditions. However, even more than the president, they want a budget that can be beaten. If they miss their budgets they know that something bad will happen, anywhere from embarrassment through having to take corrective action to being fired.

Every manager has this contradiction between planning "the best results achievable" and a budget that "will be beaten." All managers, except the lowest-level, are both superiors and subordinates in the budgeting process. As superiors, they want to challenge their subordinates to get the best performance possible, because management owes that to the owner(s). However, as subordinates, they want to make sure that they are not promising too much, with resulting loss of credibility and other problems. Since this is fundamental to any budgeting situation, this is the first inherent problem of budgeting.

Measurement

Measurement of management against financial results is so obviously appropriate that it is impossible to conceive of not doing it. Also, while not the only way, there are good arguments for tying bonuses substantially to performance versus budget. However, measurement is clearly the enemy of realistic budgeting, the second inherent problem in developing good budgets.

Because compensation and even job security are involved, managers will not plan the best results achievable, but will be as conservative as the approval process will allow. Their budgets will contain hidden pads and pockets of contingency funds. Further, budgets that could be beaten may not be. Managers will tend to ensure that all budgeted money is spent, both so that they will not be accused of submitting an unrealistic budget, and so that their funds will not be cut in the following year.

Even more fundamental are the surprises to which every business is subject. These make management difficult to measure in any sense. Often the best management jobs are done in bad years, as organizations scramble to overcome the unexpected loss of a major customer, for example. However, if the budget is used as a strong measurement criterion, that good job will not be recognized because the major customer loss will not be overcome in time to meet the budget. All managers must guard against adverse measurement of their work. The surprises that may lurk out there will make them hedge and pad their budgets, again making them less realistic than they could be.

The Uncertainty of the Future

The only sure things about the future are that things will change and there will be surprises. Managers are paid for dealing with this future uncertainty, and they never have complete information upon which to base decisions. Managers deal with uncertainty by using the best information available, by hedging their bets, and by allowing for contingencies.

Budgets, however, by their numerical and detailed nature, imply and demand specificity. Managers are not asked for a range of probable sales or costs for next year; they are asked for specific numbers. As a result, the cautious type promise poorer results than they believe are achievable, as a hedge against this inherent uncertainty. The optimistic type have unreasonable faith in the future and assume that only good things will happen. In any case, the budget is less probable than its specificity implies. If the uncertainty is not treated deliberately, it will later be difficult to decide whether good or bad results are primarily because of performance or luck.

The Uncontrollability of the Outside Environment

One of the main causes of future uncertainty is the uncontrollability of the outside environment. Many outside things have a large influence on company results: market health, competitors' actions, supplier actions, the state of the relevant economy, new laws and government regulations, tight credit, etc. Each company has its own list of important outside factors that are crucial to its success. A local retail business will be significantly affected by the closing of a nearby military base, while a company selling big-ticket items internationally can be significantly affected by changes in the value of the dollar.

The important points for budgeting are that (1) these outside environments are very important in determining next year's results, (2) the only thing certain about them is that some of them will change to a surprising degree, and therefore (3) their change is an inherent problem in budgeting realistically.

The Psychological Nature of Budgeting

The final inherent problem is that budgeting has always been, and will always be, essentially a psychological process. The boss wants the best results possible and wants the organization to be challenged, while the subordinate wants a budget that can be beaten in an uncertain and uncontrollable environment.

Both boss and subordinate must go through a mental process of estimating the other's state of mind. A simple but trivial example is the case in which the subordinate knows that the boss has arbitrarily cut everybody's submitted expenses every year by 5 percent. It does not take a Rhodes scholar to figure out that expenses in the budget should be padded by 5 percent more than the subordinate feels are needed. Real psychological games, played by both sides, are more sophisticated and complex. Each considers the other's past practices, credibility, general pessimism or optimism, etc. Each maneuvers to get the budget to the numbers that he or she believes are proper.

There is nothing sinister in this. The best possible people will have these problems; if they are good, the final compromise will probably be good. The problem is that the psychology can easily overwhelm the reality, and something far less than optimum becomes the final budget. Also, the psychological games are what usually make budgeting so painful, with long sessions, and emotion and anguish on both sides.

Conclusion: The Problems to Be Overcome

We are now in position to state why it is inherently difficult to generate good budgets. The budget deals with the next year. Many things about the next year are uncertain, because (1) it is the future, and (2) much of it is uncontrollable. About the part that can be known, the people who know best, the managers directly involved, are not motivated to be realistic in their budget submissions. The finished budget is then (usually) cast in concrete and (always) used to measure the participants.

The inherent problems will not go away; they are fundamental characteristics of any budgeting situation. They must be dealt with, neutralized, and surmounted for budgeting to have value.

One hopes they will be dealt with at the company level. ENLIGHT-

ENED, INC., has a budgeting process designed to meet the following requirements, which follow from the different objectives and the inherent problems:

- The budget must be prepared in the proper strategic context.
- The process must deal realistically with uncertainty and uncontrollability.
- The format must be selected that provides the most useful information for management.
- The content must provide the best possible numerical predictions of next year's results.
- The process must emphasize the encouragement of excellence at all levels within the company.
- A coherent, efficient, and timely process flow must tie everything together.

This process allows the budget to be changed in response to significant changes in legitimate outside uncontrollable factors. It minimizes the psychological games by promoting excellence and continuous improvement, and by focus on the most useful parameters and the best numerical content. It also accents preparatory work—the link with strategy, definition of outside factors and assumptions, identification of critical problems and improvement goals, and preliminary budgets—that minimizes the iterative number crunching.

MUDDLED, INC., allows the inherent problems full sway. It asks for numbers early, provides little guidance, and believes that budgets should never be changed. MUDDLED leaves its managers to cope with the inherent problems on their own. But cope they must, if their budgets are to be valuable and useful tools rather than a continuing problem.

Even at MUDDLED, INC., managers can do a lot to improve their own budgets by doing their planning and thinking before generating numbers. They can identify their important uncontrollable factors and make assumptions about them. They can define their outputs and firmly tie their cost and resource requirements to a given level of output. They can emphasize the most important parameters and use the best methods for numerical predictions. They can focus on important problems and push continuous improvement and excellence. They can develop a private process that does the necessary preparatory work before the company's budgeting process begins. In doing all this they must clearly communicate what they are doing, particularly assumptions and outputs, so rationality can replace emotion in their reviews.

Why Is Budgeting So Difficult? 27

How to accomplish all this is the subject of the rest of the book, wherein we come to grips with the work of budgeting.

Tips and Traps

- Remember that budgeting is fundamentally a planning activity. Plans have to take into account all relevant conditions, so budgeting plans must allow for the manifestation of these inherent problems. If you have a new superior, for example, you must particularly strive to understand his or her psychological approach to budgeting.

Part II
The Planning Work of Budgeting

4
Planning

Before planning anything, one must know what planning is, and how to plan. Since the budget is most fundamentally a plan (or more rigorously, the numerical expression of a number of related plans), planning is the first important element of budgeting work.

Everyone plans, all the time. If you wanted to go from New York to Chicago, you would not just go out your front door without any thought. You would first decide whether to go by plane, car, train, or bus. Depending on your individual needs and experience, your decision may be quick and obvious or it may require some work: collecting information on schedules, costs, comfort, and the like. This part of the planning process for your trip is analogous to a strategic plan: the choice of the general approach that will be taken to achieve one or more objectives.

Assuming you decided to go by car, you still would not just get into your car without further thought. You would first decide what route to take and whether to drive straight through or stop overnight on the way. In the latter case you would decide where to stop (or you might justifiably put off that decision until you were out on the road). You would decide how much money and what supplies to take with you. You would decide whether to have the car serviced, and so on.

You would probably not write all this down, at least not in the fancy report or presentation of a typical business plan. However, you would have decided how you were going to get to Chicago before you started the trip. This part of the planning is analogous to an action plan. The budget is the action plan for the next year.

Planning is just that simple and, at the same time, just that complex. There is no magic involved, only logical and intelligent thought. However, a plan must be a *plan*, not a miscellaneous collection of information. It must tell us how we are going to get there from here, after defining what "there" is. The following paragraphs discuss various aspects of planning in general, followed by an overview of the planning work of budgeting.

The Elements of Planning

A plan is the determination of the way resources will be used to achieve particular results. To do this, a plan must contain the following five elements, indicated in Figure 4-1:

1. *The goal*—a statement of the desired results to which the plan is addressed. The goal will change as the planning progresses. In the above simple example, the goal of the first planning stage was to go to Chicago. That decision led to another plan whose goal was to determine the best way to go to Chicago.

2. *The "what"*—everything that must be done to achieve the desired results. In the Chicago car trip these include choosing the route and deciding whether to stop overnight. "Choosing the route" implies an earlier, prerequisite activity of "getting a map." The decision of whether to stop overnight is a prerequisite to the decision of what clothes to take. And so on.

3. *The "how"*—the methods and approaches that will be used to accomplish all the things that must be done. In deciding how to go to Chicago, you might gather timetables and call airlines and railroads yourself, or you might give the whole task to a travel agent. For the car trip itself, the "how" would include the number of drivers and whether to take food or stop for meals.

Figure 4-1. The elements of planning.

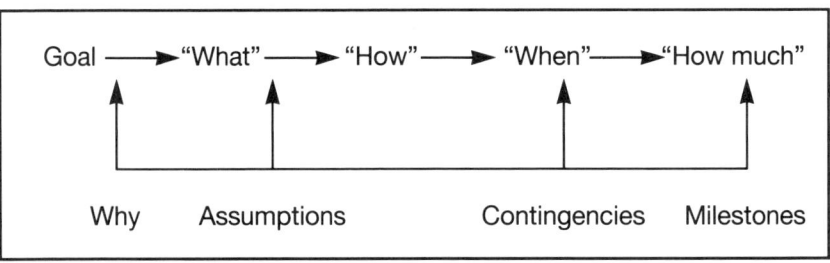

```
Goal ──▶ "What" ──▶ "How" ──▶ "When" ──▶ "How much"
          ▲          ▲          ▲          ▲
          │          │          │          │
         Why     Assumptions  Contingencies  Milestones
```

4. *The "when"*—the schedule for accomplishing all the activities and the final results. For the Chicago trip, you would start with the date and time you need to be there, working back to when the various decisions must be made. Finally, with the entire plan in hand, the departure date and time would be decided.

5. *The "how much"*—the resources required to carry out the plan: people, money, particular skills, outside purchased items, etc. Even for the simple example of the Chicago trip, you want to know the total cost, and particular things to buy, like clothes and food.

The above items are the essential elements of any plan. There are also supporting elements that most plans should contain, which allow justification, evaluation, and proper modification of plans and resulting work:

- The *"why"*—defense of the activities and schedules chosen to achieve the desired results
- The *assumptions* made in the plan
- *Contingency plans*, which will be used if assumptions prove incorrect or particular activities are unsuccessful
- *Milestones*—the dates and content of important interim results, which allow evaluation of progress versus the plan

How to Plan

The following steps provide an outline of how to plan:

- When required to prepare a plan, always start with the *goal*. Make sure that it is specific and appropriate, and that it is understood. The goal determines the type of plan and the planning activity, and it may change as planning proceeds. If you are told to prepare a plan for cutting costs, the initial work must be a search for the best areas to cut and the initial goal must be their identification. On the other hand, if you are told to prepare a plan to cut a particular cost, action planning is immediately required.
- The next step is *what* must be done. This is best done by reasoning backward from the goal to determine the major interim accomplishments needed. The main prerequisites for introduction of a new financial service are definition of the service, who will do the operations work involved and how, the initial marketing of the service, and trained

salespersons and operators. Definition of the service, in turn, requires completed testing, completed design, and pricing decisions, leading back to service specifications. After thinking through the sequence and structure of major activities, the details can be filled in.

Always express an activity in terms of its result rather than the type of work done in the activity. "Decide on the route" conveys more information than "study the map." "Decide pricing" is more useful than "analyze profitability at various volumes and prices."

- *How* to do the activities can be so simple that it practically merges into "what." The method of training salespersons might be obvious, so the approach is almost known when the need for trained salespersons is stated. On the other hand, no one will approve a product design plan unless impressed with the design concept and the approaches that will be taken to resolve fundamental uncertainties.

  In preparing a plan, the emphasis and effort to be placed on the "how" depends upon (1) what you must know *now* to be confident of successfully carrying out the plan and (2) the information that you must present to get the plan approved. If the approach for a particular activity is critical relative to either of these criteria, the effort to identify the approach must be done during planning. If not, the "how" can be left as a later decision to be made (with a suitable entry for that decision activity in the plan).

- *When* various activities and the total plan must be completed can come into play in two opposite ways. A required schedule for completion is sometimes stated with the planning assignment and goal. In that case, you must schedule backward from the end date, fitting the activities and their schedules to the required completion date. The other case is the one in which no required completion date is given, with the required schedule being one of the planning outputs. This case is a normal scheduling problem of estimating the time required for each activity, and trying to optimize the interrelationships to minimize the overall schedule.

- The key to *how much,* or the costs and resource requirements, is mainly to have thought through and identified all necessary work. Involve a financial analyst, since they are trained and experienced to recognize all the types of costs involved in an endeavor. They are also usually good at reasonableness checks on cost estimates. They can be relied upon to remember depreciation expense and to use the right burden rates (see Appendix A for an explanation of the accounting terms used in budgeting) and the right salary levels. They will not forget, as operating managers sometimes do, that benefits costs must be added to labor costs.

- **The best defense and justification of a plan, the *why*, is a good plan: with the goal fully addressed; logical, complete, and properly sequenced activities; persuasive approaches; responsive schedules; and reasonable costs.** In addition, the planner must become aware of superiors' major concerns and ensure that these are addressed.

- All but the simplest of plans should enumerate the *assumptions* made in the planning. They are vital for evaluation of the work resulting from the plan, and also for deciding periodically whether to continue or cancel the program. If assumptions are not made clear, it can be difficult to tell if problems are the result of poor work or assumptions that have been overturned by events. The subject of assumptions must be things outside the control of the workers on the project; otherwise, some of their legitimate responsibilities will be assumed away.

- Although not all plans need associated *contingency* plans, they are especially important for critical subjects, when one or more assumptions are crucial and/or when there are major uncertainties. Consider a product plan. If the company needs the product, it cannot just be canceled if things do not work out. If a technical breakthrough is needed, there should be alternative approaches in case the chosen method fails. New products often do not exactly fit the market as originally conceived; assumptions about markets are difficult to make correctly. Therefore, there also should be alternative features in mind, and built-in design flexibility, in case the assumptions have to be changed.

- Finally, all but the simplest plans should include *milestones*, to allow the planners, implementers, and bosses to continually evaluate progress as the work proceeds.

When faced with any complex planning activity, a "plan for a plan" should be prepared first. Its elements are the same as have been described here, but its goal is the plan itself. Major plans involve many people and extensive work; that planning work itself needs to be planned, scheduled, and managed.

Some Characteristics of Business Plans

Business plans have some particular characteristics (see Figure 4-2) that should be noted.

Figure 4-2. Characteristics of business plans.

Complexity
Uncertainty
Specificity
Detail

Complexity

Plans and planning in business are much more complex than a trip to Chicago, of course. Overall plans may include a number of supporting or subsidiary plans and planning stages. Most plans have many interrelated activities that must be done in the right time sequence; scheduling such complex projects is a major planning activity in itself. A major project or product plan may have hundreds of activities. Particularly in technical plans, the "how"—i.e., the design concepts and approaches to be investigated—can be most important. Finally, ensuring that all costs are included can be complicated, and the availability of particular skills can be a key issue.

To illustrate the extent and interrelations of planning in business, consider a business that has developed a strategic plan to increase penetration of a particular market. Among other things, this will lead to plans for various new products and/or services. For every new product or service, the first planning stage is to determine the requirements that it must meet. This will be followed by plans for design, production, marketing, sales, service, and perhaps such things as recruiting and capital equipment. Good planning always includes feedback among the stages, allowing, for example, cost and reliability considerations to influence design and even requirements.

Uncertainty

All plans include uncertainty by definition, because they deal with the future. The uncertainty makes planning more important, not less. A smart person once said, "Plans are nothing, but planning is everything." As conditions change, plans must change. A plan is a "stake in the ground," which tells an organization where it is and where it is going. It must know both in order to evaluate intelligently when to change what it is doing. This is the reason for including assumptions in plans, and for doing contingency planning for the important assumptions. Plans must include enough latitude and contingencies to accommodate a reasonable range of uncertainty. In the meantime, an organization must know what it will be doing today and tomorrow.

A bank branch manager must plan the number of tellers to employ, subject to an implicit or explicit requirement that strikes some balance between customer waiting time and bank cost. The manager never knows how many customers will actually come in on a particular day next March. He or she plans on the basis of an expected range of the number of customers per day. The plan also possibly includes a provision for drafting other bank employees into temporary service as tellers to handle an unexpected peak. The plan itself would not be changed until data over a period of time show that the general daily level of customers is higher or lower than expected. The manager would not know when to change the level of teller staffing unless a plan had been developed for a particular service and cost goal, with the customer level assumed. Without a plan, the only alternative might be to hire and fire frequently.

Specificity

Every plan should be specific, even the most general, highest-level plan. There must be a specific goal. The goal of a product plan cannot be to develop either product A or product B. That defines two plans, one for each. Further, the product plan goal cannot be, "Increase market share." That implies a preliminary planning stage whose purpose is to determine how to increase market share, which may later lead to one or more product plans.

Similarly, other planning elements must be specific. Responsibility for a design or other activity cannot be given to two organizations, or no organization. Even if it proves to be a gross approximation, an expected cost or reasonable range of costs should be given. Planners seldom have complete information about necessary activities when a plan is prepared. In that case, it is both valid and necessary for the plan to state that a particular decision must be made, when it must be made, and the activities and considerations involved in making it. If the nature of the decision, the date, and the considerations are stated, the plan is still specific.

Detail

The amount of detail, however, is another story. There are two dimensions over which detail should vary greatly. The first is the organizational level for which the plan is prepared. A plan prepared by the president may include only the amount of orders expected. The sales manager, however, needs to know how those orders will be obtained and the most likely potential customers. Each organizational level needs the amount of detail required for it to do its work and to judge the plan.

The second dimension that determines appropriate detail is time—the period addressed by the plan. The shorter the term of the plan, the more detail it must contain to be useful. A plan for sales calls for next week should identify each customer who will be visited. A similar plan for the fourth quarter of next year should only list the expected number of sales calls per week, in most cases with no identification at all. One cannot know which specific prospects should be called upon during the fourth quarter; nor does one need the information now. What the salesperson or sales manager needs to know now about next year's fourth quarter are the number of calls expected to be made, the number of resulting orders, and the associated cost.

Thus the guiding principles for the amount of detail in planning are to include only what is known, what is needed at the present time, and what is needed by the level of those involved in carrying out the plan. Excessive detail clutters a plan and detracts from its primary message. On the other hand, if less detail is available than is needed, more data must be generated before the plan can be completed. If the sales manager notes that one of the salespersons cannot identify prospects for sales calls next week, that identification becomes a prerequisite of the plan.

Consideration of detail illustrates how related families of plans exist in business planning. A three-year plan needs little detail, but each year an annual plan is probably needed to flesh it out. Similarly, quarterly, monthly, or even weekly plans are then needed to flesh out the annual plan.

Bad Planning

Sadly, too many plans in business seem to be designed to impress the reader with the writer's knowledge of the subject, rather than to tell the reader what will be *done*. They are long, impressive documents with erudite discussions of applicable theory and principles, but are short on

Planning

results and activities. Project proposals particularly seem to exhibit such characteristics.

Assume that you want to build a house. Your desired result will be a certain number of rooms and particular features, plus a desired cost range or maximum. You will not let the builder start your house on the basis of a discussion demonstrating how much he or she knows about houses, plus some general ideas about your house. You will require plans, drawings, schedules, a rendering of the completed house, and cost estimates that will exactly describe the house to be built for you. You will probably let the builder start before every single decision is made, but you will carefully note what decisions remain and when they must be made to keep the construction on schedule.

Keep the house example in mind when you are required to plan anything. It will not be sufficient to impress your superior with what you know; you must convey to him or her what you will *do*.

The Planning Work of Budgeting: Overview

This discussion of the general world of planning provides a context for the planning work of budgeting (see Figure 4-3). In this case the overall period for the plan is given: the next year. Reduced to essentials, the budget asks each manager the question "What outputs can your organization achieve next year at what cost, and what particular resources are required?"

The planning goal of budgeting is, narrowly, the prediction of the financial statements—profit and loss, balance sheet, and cash flow—for next year. More broadly, that ultimate goal is *adequate* numerical results in those financial statements. How much is adequate depends on company investment and the internal and external conditions that determine what is possible.

To develop the prediction of next year's financial statements, the overall working goal is to predict revenue and all the kinds of costs that the company will incur to produce that revenue. The costs will then be converted into the proper accounting category—expense, capital expenditures, inventory, prepaid expense, etc.—which, together with things like payment and collection times, translate revenue and all costs into the financial statements.

However, revenue is not properly an organizational output. In the sense of the work to be done, revenue is a by-product of products shipped, services delivered, and the like. Further, many individual organizations within the company have outputs that do not directly

Figure 4-3. The elements of planning in budgeting.

Goal	To predict organization outputs, costs, and needs from other organizations
"What" and "How"	1. Defining the organization's work: inputs, activities, outputs, output dictators, and cost drivers
	2. Planning continuous performance improvement
"When" and Milestones	Schedules of inputs, activities, and outputs
"How Much"	Costs and needs from other organizations
"Why"	Justification that results in budget approval (see Chapter 14)
Assumptions	Explicit budgeting assumptions
Contingency Plans	Generally implicit—part of getting the budget approved

relate to revenue: purchased material for purchasing, product designs for engineering, monthly financial reports for accounting, etc. Thus *the actual planning goal of budgeting for each manager is to predict organization outputs, costs, and needs from other organizations.*

Between the broad ultimate goal of satisfactory numbers and the working goal for each manager, there will be multiple iterations. Before the planning, no one is smart enough to know what the organization can accomplish next year. Much of the work and grief of budgeting involves reconciling managers' planning goals with the financial needs of the company.

The next step in the planning work of budgeting is to define the organization's work. The only proper way to do this is in terms of its outputs, inputs, and activities. Visualize your organization as the flow chart shown in Figure 4-4.

The activities, what the organization *does* to transform the inputs into outputs, are the "what" and "how" of the planning work of budgeting. Some inputs come from outside the company, but most usually come from other company organizations. That is, one organization's output is another organization's input. Thus organization inputs

Figure 4-4. Organization work flow.

```
Inputs  →→→  [ Activities ]  →→→  Outputs
```

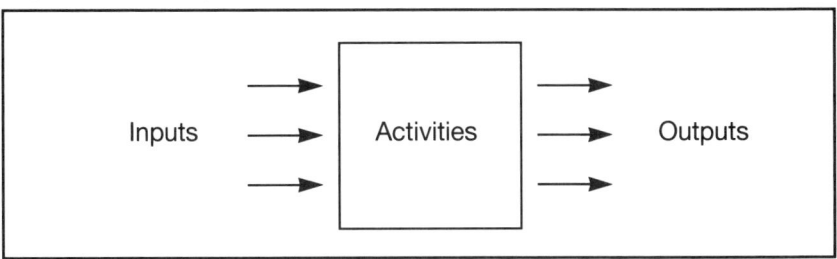

are synonymous with part of the goal statement: "needs from other organizations."

Outputs, inputs, and activities define the organization's work in a narrow sense, but an additional step is needed for useful understanding. Managers must know what determines their outputs and costs, and thus where to get the information they will need to put numbers into their budgets. Thus the definition of the organization's work should include determination of its output dictators and cost drivers. Output dictators are covered together with outputs in Chapter 5. Since most of the detailed work of budgeting is concerned with costs, Chapter 6 is devoted to the nature of business costs, cost relationships, and, most important, cost drivers.

Unfortunately but universally, not all the required inputs and outputs for the next year can be known during budgeting. This is mostly due to the uncertainty of the future and the uncontrollability of the outside environment. It also stems from business and procedural decisions made in other parts of the company, affecting a particular manager's work, but beyond his or her influence or control. Output and input uncertainties unavoidably are handled by assumptions, implicit or explicit. Chapter 7 argues that assumptions should be explicit, and presents a process for making proper assumptions. The assumptions process is a powerful tool in dealing with uncertainty, the cause of many of the deficiencies of budgeting. If MUDDLED, INC., installed an assumptions process and did nothing else, it would see marked improvement in its budgets and management.

A final step still remains in the planning work of budgeting. All managers have the obligation to encourage excellence, to seek continuous performance improvement within their organizations and across neighboring organizations. If the planning work of budgeting is done right—that is, by defining the work and using assumptions to cope with uncertainty—the budgeting process is both the natural and ideal time to focus on such performance improvements. An excellent tool for doing this, within your own organization or across organizations, is gap analysis, the subject of Chapter 8.

Gap analysis will lead to further, desirable iterations of the budgeting cycle. Those involving one's own organization will change only activities. However, the real payoffs come from those involving multiple organizations, which can change a given organization's outputs, inputs, and activities, resulting in better performance/cost relationships for the company.

With the organization's work thus defined and necessary assumptions made, the manager is ready to lay out and schedule the work for next year, yielding the planning goal of outputs, costs, and needs from other organizations. See Figure 4-5. The manager starts with identification of type and amount of required outputs, helped by knowledge of the output dictators, and makes assumptions for those that are unknown. These determine the amount and type of needed activities, and the resulting needed inputs (which may also require some assumptions). The organization's costs, determined from the cost drivers, then flow directly from the activities, while needs from other organizations flow from the inputs required.

There is iteration, of course, not shown in Figure 4-5. First, the availability of different forms of inputs will change the activities. Second, the level and kind of required outputs may change as the budget is consolidated and reworked, and as other organizations specify differ-

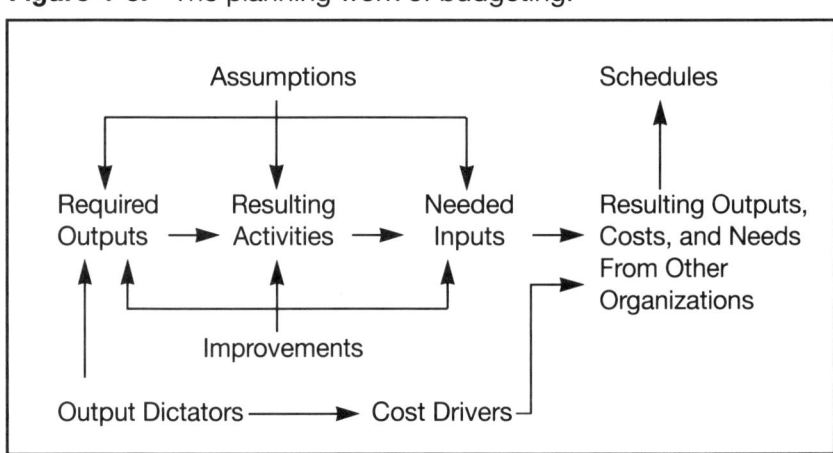

Figure 4-5. The planning work of budgeting.

ent needs from the subject organization. Finally, the required level of outputs might not be achievable because of resource and capability limitations. Therefore, "resulting outputs" might be different from "required outputs," starting another iteration rippling through the company.

The resulting schedule of each output, input, and activity is then the "when" of the manager's planning. The costs and needs numbers are the "how much." The way to generate the best numbers in predicting next year is a major subject in itself, and is the subject of Part III.

The next four chapters will discuss the elements of planning the organization's work in more detail: defining the work, costs and cost drivers, assumptions, and gap analysis.

Two Questions

Before proceeding, let us answer two questions that may be in the minds of some readers.

1. "Why do all this planning? I just add up the costs that I have and maybe increase a few."
2. "Why do all this planning when we never know next year's outputs anyway? We always have to guess."

The reason for doing the planning is to understand the work to be done and what gives rise to the organization's costs. This lets the manager determine the best way to achieve the outputs, the best activities and resources to use. It gives the manager the basis to improve things, thereby achieving more output and/or reducing costs. It enables him or her to react quickly to changes in required outputs, either as budgeting progresses or during the next year. It keeps the manager from being surprised by unanticipated information or service outputs. In short, the planning enables the manager to improve performance and to react to the changes that will surely occur. These characteristics are a large part of the definition of a good manager, as well as a good budgeter.

How else can you survive a critical review? How else can you either implement or argue against a personnel cut, so common these days? How else can you find better ways to do things? And, if you cannot do any of these things, how will you ever get promoted?

Tips and Traps

- Don't get hung up on the mystique or jargon of planning. Concentrate on the needed information, which is determined by the purpose of the plan.

- Remember that a plan must be what you are going to *do*, not a chance to impress people with your knowledge. Restrict information presented to that necessary to justify and sell the plan. Besides antagonizing busy people, extraneous information might be a red herring that diverts attention from the plan that you want approved. When planners try to impress with what they *know*, their audience usually concludes that they are not quite sure what they are going to *do*.

- Never totally separate planning from implementation in your organization. The people who have to carry out a plan must believe in it and be committed to its goals, schedules, and costs. To ensure this, these same people must have a major role in the planning. Never, never let one person prepare another person's budget.

5
Defining the Organization's Work

Figure 5-1. The planning work of budgeting.

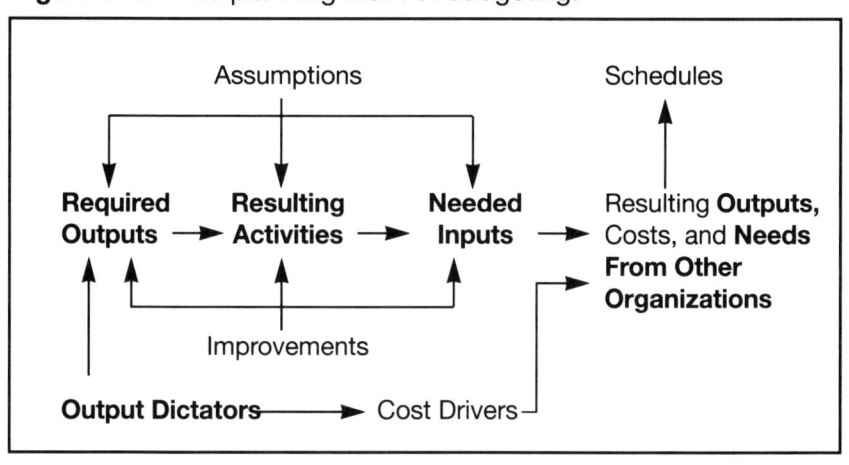

```
                    Assumptions                    Schedules
                         │                             ▲
              ┌──────────┼──────────┐                  │
              ▼          ▼          ▼
         Required    Resulting    Needed       Resulting Outputs,
         Outputs  → Activities →  Inputs    →  Costs, and Needs
              ▲          ▲          ▲            From Other
              │          │          │            Organizations
              │      Improvements   │
              │                     │
         Output Dictators ───────► Cost Drivers ┘
```

The first element of the planning work of budgeting is to define the organization's work. The proper way to do this is in terms of its inputs, outputs, and activities. Each is affected by, and affects, both of the others. Their nature should be understood before budgeting begins, so concentration can immediately be placed on their amounts for next year. That nature is the subject of this chapter; how best to estimate amounts is covered in Part III.

To complete the definition of work, managers must also understand what dictates their outputs and what drives their costs. Output dictators are covered in this chapter, while the nature of business costs and cost drivers is the subject of Chapter 6. (An example of putting all these elements together to plan an organization's work is presented at the end of Chapter 6.) The factors in the work definition that are described in this chapter are boldfaced in Figure 5-1.

This definition of inputs, outputs, output dictators, activities, and cost drivers is the *only* way to truly understand the work of an organization.

Most organizations have more inputs, outputs, and activities than are recognized intuitively. The outputs of a payroll organization are timely paychecks for every employee, in the right amount, with the correct deductions withheld; all the correct records needed for business, tax, and employee purposes; submission of all required payroll tax returns; and satisfaction of inquiries and complaints. Its inputs are pay and deduction instructions, charging instructions, time records, computer programs, data entry procedures, and general company policies and procedures. Its activities include reviewing and entering time records, reviewing payroll data prepared by the computer, entering changes in salaries and deductions, correcting errors, making adjustments, delivering paychecks, preparing tax returns, and handling inquiries. In common with every organization, there is another activity that can be called "administration": training, coaching, communication, compliance, etc.

The lists might seem surprisingly long for something as conceptually simple as a payroll function, and some may have been missed. The particulars of an organization's work are unique to every organization, and defining them is not trivial.

Organization Activities

Activities are what an organization *does*. Beyond planning the work, the importance of activities in budgeting is that an organization's costs result directly from them. Activities are central to the planning work of budgeting.

Activities are not emphasized enough in current management practices. The complexity of modern business requires elaborate organizations and procedures. Unfortunately, discussion and actions then tend to follow these organizational and procedural lines. The statement "I am in sales" does not tell you what a person does, except in a gross sense. Similarly, the statement "I think we should cut sales expense by 10 percent" does not tell you which sales expenses the speaker thinks are too high. Activity statements convey more information: "I make cold calls and sales presentations on products A, B, and C throughout the

Defining the Organization's Work

state of Ohio," or "I think we can cut the expense of cold calling by centralized telemarketing, without loss of effectiveness."

Consider material flow into a factory. The functions involved may be material management, quality control, and accounting. The material flow and associated costs can be discussed, managed, and budgeted in terms of these functions, and a material overhead rate. However, much more information is contained in descriptions of the activities involved: receive material, inspect material, move material, store material, pay for material, and supply material to assembly. Discussion in activity terms gives a better basis for managing the work, improving performance, predicting costs, and reducing costs.

An activity is the way a business employs its resources (labor, materials, time, information, and technology) to produce particular outputs. Activities can be said to be composed of tasks, processes, and operations. Rather than getting confused by the semantics of an activity versus a task, think in terms of hierarchies of activities. "Prepare reports" can be viewed as containing the subsidiary activities of "creating reports" and "typing reports." Choose the level in such a hierarchy that is useful in managing and involves significant work and costs. "Typing reports" would be significant for a word-processing organization, but not for an engineering function. The latter might even choose to move up the activity hierarchy a level above "prepare reports," to "design products," "modify products," "solve product manufacturability problems," "maintain configuration control," etc. That is, preparing reports might be considered a subsidiary activity within the main engineering activities on which its manager wishes to focus.

Most organizations have activities that are necessary but difficult to relate to particular outputs: general support activities, things that do not vary much with output, and things that are incidental to its main responsibilities. The principle of diminishing returns applies: the important thing is to define and relate high-cost and highly variable activities to outputs. An "other" category is useful and permissible for less significant activities. Also, every organization should have something like "administration" to cover incidental activities not worth delineating separately, such as training and education.

The activities that an organization must perform are determined primarily by its required outputs, but also by inputs. (The *way* it performs them is a management decision regarding processes and procedures.) For the payroll function, automation of time records would eliminate or change review, data entry, and error correction activities. The extent and amount of advertising and sales literature from the marketing department changes the activities of a sales organization. In the same way, a decision to change activities will change the inputs which an organization needs (and thus change another organization's required outputs). A printed circuit-board assembly function that switches from manual to automatic insertion will require different equipment, programming, and instructions from manufacturing engineering, and different component packaging from purchasing.

Outputs

There are many types of business organizations with many kinds of outputs. The primary outputs usually follow rather simply from the organization's function: assembled products from an assembly function, orders from a sales function, paychecks from a payroll function, customers served from a restaurant operation, copies from a reproduction center, products shipped from a divisional profit center, etc.

The next step must be the specifications that complete the description of the primary outputs. For the assembly function, these include specifications of the products assembled and the required quality level. For the sales organization, they include the products sold and the geographical area or market in which they are sold. The paychecks from the payroll function must be on time and correct in gross amounts, deductions, and net amounts. And so on.

Beyond these primary outputs, every organization has information outputs. These are dictated by outside requirements, company procedures, and the like. The assembly function must provide time records by project for its personnel, records of output achieved, reports of usage and storage of toxic materials, etc. The sales function must report its sales calls and submit travel expense reports. The payroll function must prepare and submit payroll tax returns. Plans, budgets, material requests, and such are required from most organizations.

All organizations also have what we can call service outputs. They must satisfy inquiries and complaints, provide expertise to sister organizations in solution of problems, and the like. Sales, factory, and service people all have expert advice to give on design and features of new products.

Ordinarily, the primary outputs are the main determinants of activities and costs, but not always. In some cases, information outputs—compliance with federal environmental, safety, and tax regulations—can add considerable effort and cost. Important outputs are not necessarily only the obvious ones, which is why deliberate analysis and observations are needed.

Output Dictators

Once an organization's outputs are defined, the next task is to determine what dictates those outputs so that you will know where the numbers that define next year's budget can be obtained. Also, consideration of categories of output dictators will serve as a checklist in ensuring that all outputs have been identified.

Some organizations have outputs dictated directly by orders, contract, or revenue. Examples are an engineering organization devoted to customer development contracts, a service function devoted to customer maintenance contracts, and most sales organizations.

More typical are organization outputs that are dictated by derivatives of revenue. Factories generally have a planning function that schedules all factory operations. Assembly, test, and machine shop organizations have their outputs defined by these schedules rather than directly by revenue. For organizations whose transactions generate revenue—cashing checks, selling a security, or switching telephone calls—the transaction itself is the proper output that determines the work, rather than the revenue involved.

For organizations involved in the chain of activities that generates revenue, these revenue derivatives are the most prominent dictators of primary outputs. For example:

Output Dictators	*Types of Organizations*
Production schedules	Manufacturing, engineering
Operations schedules	Operations
Maintenance schedules	Engineering, service
Transactions	Operations, accounting
Back orders	Purchasing

The origin of these revenue derivative output dictators is found in the fundamental business decisions of the company: which products and services to offer, and how to implement them. A new product decision may affect the outputs of many organizations: engineering, manufacturing, sales, purchasing, contract administration, etc.

The next logical category is outside requirements, independent of revenue. Legal and regulatory requirements dictate company outputs: annual and quarterly reports, compliance with equal employment opportunity and environmental regulations, customs and tariff regulations, and the like. Markets dictate outputs: Government procurement regulations and procurement practices in different industries dictate the information that proposals and quotations must contain. Competition can dictate outputs: Witness all the discount arrangements that airlines feel compelled to offer.

Then there are organizations whose outputs are dictated by structural factors, independent of sales except in a gross sense. These dictators are a result of the physical, procedural, and organizational way in which the company does business. The way a company is organized fundamentally establishes the responsibilities and outputs of all its component organizations. A reorganization can change them, giving a particular function a new set of "customers."

However, there is more to structural output dictators than organization. The mere fact of locations in a number of states and countries dictates a set of shipping, tax return, and communication outputs. A two-hour response requirement dictates an output for a customer service function that is dependent not on revenue but on location of customers. The outputs of a security-guard organization might be defined by the numbers of stations and hours to be covered. Establishment of a new distribution warehouse will change the geographical outputs of existing warehouses.

Finally, there are organizations whose outputs are dictated by requests for service. Their outputs are determined simply by the demands of their "customers," and they might be called "level of effort" functions. Reproduction, word processing, art departments, and the part of a facilities organization that handles office modification and rearrangement are examples of such functions. (The amount of their outputs is often unpredictable in any useful budgeting sense. "Customers" should be queried on expectations, but budgeting for such organizations often comes down to defining a capacity to serve. Sometimes that capacity is dictated by higher management as a cost control mechanism.)

In practice, one organization might have outputs of all the above types. A purchasing organization in a manufacturing department might have primary outputs dictated directly by pass-through revenue, production schedules, and inventory policy; an information requirement to report on the proportion of orders placed with small or minority businesses; and a service requirement to fulfill random headquarters purchasing needs.

Do not waste time arguing over which category an output is in. A requirement for particular proposal information is arguably dictated by either a company business decision, and therefore a derivative of revenue, or by the market. That proposal information might be a primary output for some, an information output for others. The point is to define

Defining the Organization's Work   *51*

all the organization's outputs *specifically*, and to know what dictates them. The purpose of classifying outputs and output dictators is simply to supply guidance in identifying all the outputs and their dictators.

Inputs

There are essentially three kinds of organizational inputs:

1. The things on which the organization operates, which we will call the material. These are the things that are traditionally considered inputs to any activity, in the narrow definition of the term. For an assembly organization it is the material to be assembled, for an engineering function a new product requirement or a problem to be solved, for payroll it is the time records.

2. The things from other functions that help an organization conduct its activities. These are the tools, assistance, or support. Examples are computer programs, candidates for employment from human resources, artwork, and actual tools.

3. The things that prescribe how an organization will do its work, the instructions. Examples are drawings, data entry procedures, bills of material, and policies and procedures.

Consider a sales organization. Its material inputs are the products and services to be sold (for its orders responsibility) and identification of current customers (for its customer relations responsibility). Tools inputs can be advertising and sales promotion, proposals and quotations prepared by engineering, management visits, financing arrangements, and contract forms. Instructions include price lists and allowable terms and conditions, antitrust policies, order-entry procedures, and expense account rules for entertaining customers.

The material inputs can be physical things, such as component parts for assembly, faulty equipment for maintenance service, cash for a banking transaction, and the goods to be sold in a retail store. It can also be information, evidenced by paper or bits stored in a computer. Information is probably the more common input to business organizations: all the activity records that are accounting's inputs, product descriptions for sales, product requirements for engineering, material requests for purchasing, signed applications for insurance rating and pricing, etc. In the same way, tools can be physical things or information. Instructions are always information.

Every organizational input is another organization's output, all the way back to the company's objectives and strategies. Even the raw material which comes in the back door is an output of purchasing, whose input was a bill of material from planning, whose input was a design from engineering, whose input was a product requirement from marketing, whose input was a marketing plan, whose input was the company's strategic plan.

Defining an Organization's Work

We are ready to use activities, outputs, and inputs to define the work of an organization. Most managers will find it useful to construct a flow chart, such as the one in Figure 5-2, that shows all three and their relationships.

For an existing organization, the process of capturing the way things are currently done is neither more nor less than thorough observation and recording. Start with the outputs, listing first the primary outputs and the specifications which complete their description. Then think through the information and service outputs. Finally, refer to the categories of output dictators to ensure that nothing has been missed. All outputs must be identified for a complete definition of the organization's work. Some outputs are not obvious without considerable thought.

Next, think through each input and activity involved in generating

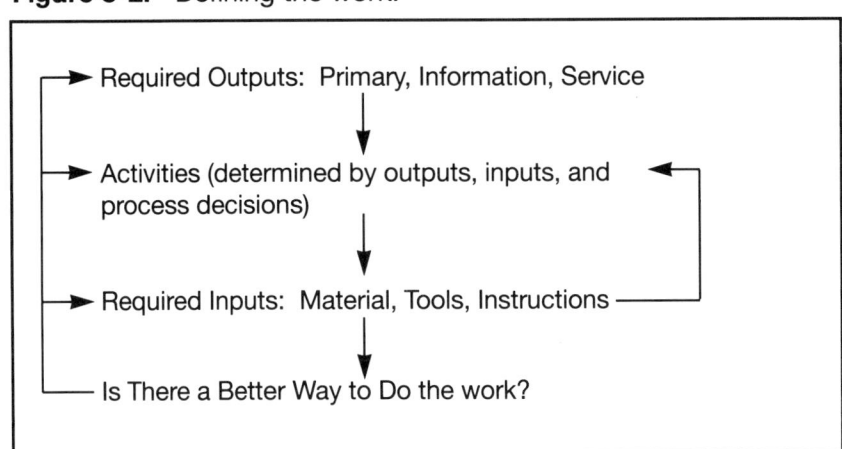

Figure 5-2. Defining the work.

```
┌─▶ Required Outputs: Primary, Information, Service
│               │
│               ▼
├─▶ Activities (determined by outputs, inputs, and  ◀─┐
│   process decisions)                                │
│               │                                     │
│               ▼                                     │
├─▶ Required Inputs: Material, Tools, Instructions ───┘
│               │
│               ▼
└── Is There a Better Way to Do the work?
```

Defining the Organization's Work

each of the outputs thus identified. The work required to produce the output should be identified first, and grouped into significant and manageable activities. Then the inputs used for each of the identified activities should be determined by asking the following questions:

> What are the materials, physical or informational, on which we must operate, or that we must transform, to achieve this output?
> What tools, assistance, and support do we need to do this?
> What instructions do we need?

The result of the above process is the definition of the organization's work, using current methods and procedures.

The remaining task for an existing organization is to answer the question "Is there a better way to do the work?" Are there other activities and inputs that will give better performance and/or lower costs in accomplishing the outputs? Also, since your organization's output is another function's input, are there different outputs that will improve company performance or reduce company costs? For example, introducing a zero defects quality responsibility into an assembly operation changes its output in terms of quality and eliminates inspections by a separate quality control organization. Inputting photos of car damage into a computer network simplifies the approval of claims at headquarters (and requires new tools—optical scanners and software—and new instructions for the adjuster). Chapter 8 describes the recommended tool for seeking the better way to do things.

When existing organizations are presented with requirements for new outputs, the process of defining the work is one of design rather than observation. This is natural and common management work: Given a new output, what work (activities) will we do to accomplish it, and what inputs will we need? (Interestingly, this design is always done for new outputs, but things that have been done for years are often difficult to describe, and the reasons for doing them a certain way even harder to remember.)

Finally, a new organization must define the work from scratch, and this is the manager's first task. Presumably, primary outputs are always given, but not always specified and described completely. These specifications, plus the required information and service outputs, must be sought as the organization moves into operation. The activities and inputs must be determined almost simultaneously. This takes considerable work, and is often a trial-and-error process over time. The process will be easier if it is approached deliberately as a definition of the work, as advocated here.

Preparation for budgeting a new organization will naturally involve uncertainty, because the work will not yet be fully defined. The work definition and subsequent work plans should be developed as fully as possible. Then assumptions (Chapter 7) should be used to cover the uncertainties. The latter not only transmit the best information to all concerned but constitute a checklist for the information still needed to define the new organization.

Tips and Traps

- Different things done in other organizations will change a given organization's inputs and outputs, and therefore its activities. Most problems are interfunctional or interorganization problems. Most progress is made by finding better ways to do things across functions and organizations.

- Definition of organization work in this manner is also useful in planning or considering reorganizations. Whenever you are either a reorganizer or a reorganizee, life will be simpler if inputs, outputs, and activities of each organization involved are defined and documented. This should be done before and after the reorganization. It will help in the decision, in the transition, and in making sure that nothing falls through the cracks.

6
Understanding Costs and Cost Drivers

Figure 6-1. The planning work of budgeting.

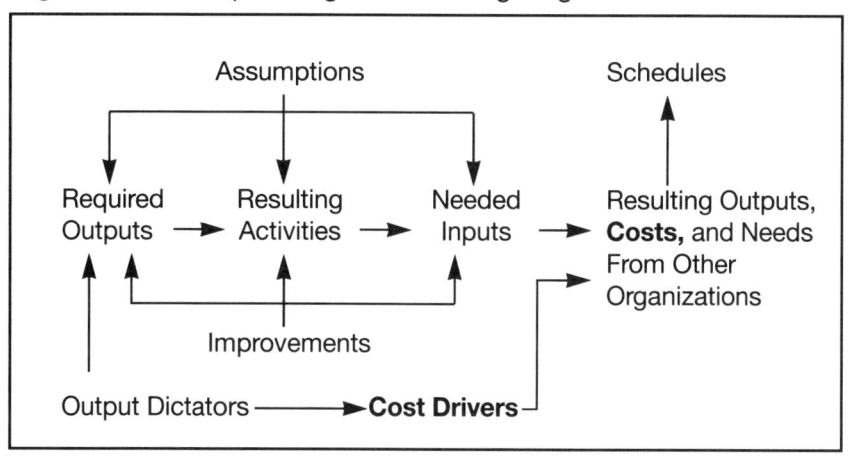

```
                    Assumptions                    Schedules
                         │                             ▲
         ┌───────┬───────┼───────┐                     │
         ▼       ▼       ▼                             │
      Required  Resulting  Needed      Resulting Outputs,
      Outputs → Activities → Inputs →  Costs, and Needs
         ▲       ▲          ▲          From Other
         │       │          │          Organizations
         │       Improvements
         │
      Output Dictators ──────► Cost Drivers
```

Most of the work of budgeting revolves around costs. There are essentially four things that managers need to know about costs relative to budgeting:

1. The nature of the costs their organizations will incur, plus the way the company groups these costs and the definition of terms used for them.
2. The inherent relationships among certain kinds of costs—that is, costs that are unavoidably affected if another cost is changed.
3. The things that drive the costs. Cost drivers are fundamental to understanding and planning the work.
4. How to estimate and predict costs.

55

The first three are covered in this chapter. How to estimate and predict costs is the subject of Chapter 11. The cost factors relative to budgeting that are described in this chapter are boldfaced in Figure 6-1.

The Nature of Business Costs

The first concern relative to costs is simply the types of costs that must be incurred by the organization to carry out its responsibilities. This is a management question, not an accounting question. However, it quickly involves accounting, because managers also need to know how their costs will be grouped, reported, and measured. Therefore, the coverage of the nature of costs includes discussion of their accounting treatment. (See Appendix A, The Language of Accounting and Appendix B, Glossary of Accounting Terms Used in Budgeting.)

There are a number of ways to categorize business costs. A straightforward way to discuss them is to divide costs into things that the company *makes* or does, and things that the company *buys*.

The costs of things that the company makes or does are labor and associated costs. The labor costs are salaries, wages, commissions, bonuses, and such things as overtime premiums, if applicable. The costs associated with labor are the various things that are generally called benefits, such as vacation and holiday pay, sick pay, and insurance. Conventionally, if outside contractors are used to accomplish work, rather than employees, that is a "bought" cost.

Thus the nature of "make" costs is simple. Unfortunately the accounting treatment is not. As discussed in Appendix A, different types of business account for labor costs quite differently. For example:

- In some retail businesses and many small businesses, labor costs are simply the salaries of the employees.

- Manufacturing businesses generally wish to keep track of their direct expense, to know the profitability of their various products. To do that, time spent on (charged to) direct labor on each project or product must be known, and time records are kept of how employees spend and charge their time. Employees are often labeled as direct or indirect. The indirect people—all general and administrative people, managers, engineers, planners, secretaries—ordinarily charge their time to indirect labor. The direct people also have idle time, training time, and the like, which gives rise to a category often called "indirect of direct."

- In an engineering organization that works on customer contracts, internally funded product development, and sales proposals, the first two are ordinarily direct labor, while the last is indirect. The operative difference is that direct costs are burdened in some way with overhead charges while indirect are not.

- Service companies vary from simple "labor cost equals salaries" to complete project accounting similar to that used in a factory. It depends upon the type of service and the way it is billed. Financial service companies and personal service firms generally follow the simple path. Maintenance service and project companies ordinarily follow the complex path.
- Some distribution companies compute cost of sales and gross margin, but, unlike manufacturers, only include material costs therein. All labor costs are considered, in effect, indirect expense.

For companies that break down labor costs into direct and indirect, the remainder of salary and wage costs—vacations, holidays, sick time—ordinarily goes into benefits expense. In businesses where the labor costs are not subdivided, vacations and the like are probably included in salaries; benefits expense, then, is only the insurance and other things the company buys.

The importance of things that a company buys varies with business, management, and time. For example, office supplies are a minor category for manufacturing businesses, and may just be included in the "other indirect" category. However, a word processing bureau probably budgets and tracks office supplies as a significant expense. If management of any company gets concerned about any expense, it will soon be budgeted and tracked separately, to give its control the desired emphasis.

The most important things that businesses buy are those things directly related to revenue. In retail and distribution businesses, the things sold are generally identical to the things bought. The same thing is true of a bank, which primarily buys and sells money. Other financial services businesses, such as insurance companies, also "buy" and "sell" money in some form.

In manufacturing businesses, raw materials, components, and subassemblies are bought and turned into products by labor. In utilities, systems and equipment and either fuel, power, or raw materials are bought and turned into delivered services (electricity, telecommunications, gas, water, etc.) through labor. For maintenance service businesses, the comparable things bought are tools, spare parts, shop equipment, and perhaps trucks.

These various things bought that are directly related to sales are called by different names in different businesses. The most common term in manufacturing businesses is "direct material." In retailing and distribution they are usually called "inventory" or "stock." The money that a bank buys is its "capital" and "liabilities."

Then again, there are businesses that buy nothing directly related to sales. These are personal service firms—lawyers, consultants, agents and brokers of all kinds.

Most companies buy things that are investments necessary to produce revenue or generally to conduct business. These include factory and store equipment, buildings or improvements to leased facilities, tools, computers, trucks, etc. These are ordinarily accounted for as capital expenditures, and budgeted and recorded separately. Capital expenditures are discussed in Chapter 12.

All companies have other things they buy to conduct their businesses, often called support costs or costs of doing business:

- *Personnel-related:* memberships, subscriptions, travel and living, training courses, etc. Most of these are related to increasing knowledge and information and thus to the skills and value of the work force.

- *Facilities-related:* rent, utilities, maintenance and repair, security guards, etc. If the facilities are owned, there will be depreciation and amortization rather than rent. Improvements to facilities are usually capital expenditures, whether the facility is owned or leased. In the latter case, they are usually called "leasehold improvements."

- *Outside services:* consultants, legal expense, design and drafting services, temporary personnel.

- *Other:* advertising and sales promotion, taxes, board of directors costs, freight, contributions, and the like.

With these general categories and examples as guides, managers must learn the specific elements of their organization's costs. Involve the budget analyst to ensure that you are aware of all types of costs your organization incurs. Budget analysts are experienced and trained to recognize all the types of costs involved in an endeavor. They are also the best source of how the different costs are grouped and treated by accounting.

Cost Relationships

The second thing that the manager needs to know about costs is the relationships among certain costs. If there is a given amount of work to be done, some costs unavoidably increase if others are cut. Further, if the current way is the most efficient way, total costs will increase if one of the cost elements is arbitrarily cut.

Consider an old favorite of managements everywhere: an arbitrary cut of the number of employees. If the amount of work has not changed, the employee reductions must be made up by using outside contractors. If using employees was the most efficient way to do the work, the substitution of outside contractors for employees will increase the overall costs. Thus labor costs will indeed be less as a result of this arbitrary cut, but "outside services" will increase by more than labor costs decrease.

The only ways to cut costs are to find more efficient ways to do a given amount of work, or to do less work. Managers need to guard against the illusion that cutting one element of cost $X will produce $X overall savings, if the work is not changed. To be able to budget and manage realistically, managers must understand their unavoidable cost relationships. This must come from the understanding of their work, but here are some generally applicable examples:

- If there is a given amount of remote work to be done—selling, customer contact, working with project partners, dealing with a department in a distant city, etc.—travel and telecommunications expense cannot both be reduced. If managers cut travel expense, they must expect telecommunications expense to increase.

- For a given amount of work to be done, overtime costs will rise if the number of employees is reduced. The opposite should also be true.

- The cost of high-priced professional people necessarily includes costs of things that keep them current in their professions, such as memberships, seminars, courses, books, and magazines. If the business needs these professional people, management must accept that such supporting expenses are necessary costs of doing business.

Cost Drivers

The third thing that managers need to know about costs is the things that cause or drive them. This is the last step in defining the organization's work, the most important thing to know about costs if they are to be planned and budgeted intelligently. Knowledge of cost drivers is also important in evaluating changes during the budgeting process, and also changes in plans during the course of the budget year. That knowledge allows managers to understand quickly whether such changes will have major or minor effects, whether they require quick reaction or can be taken in stride.

The most important use of the knowledge of cost drivers is not in budgeting but in improving organizational performance. The cost drivers show where to look for the biggest improvement payoffs. These days a small manufacturer can find that costs (and risks) of the paint shop are strongly driven by environmental regulations. It may pay to "buy" painting if the painting operation is small. Similarly, the amount of costs driven simply by the existence of manual time records can be an eye opener leading to automation of those time records.

In general, organizational costs are driven by required outputs, by procedures and processes used, and by general price levels.

Required outputs are an obvious cost driver. Usually, the more products assembled or engineering changes made and processed, the higher will be the costs. Also, output complexity and diversity will make costs higher. Changing output requirements to specify higher performance products will increase purchased material and manufacturing costs.

The characteristics of required outputs that drive cost are generally identical with the output dictators discussed in Chapter 5: revenue, derivatives of revenue, outside requirements, structural factors, and requests for service. For additional examples from each category, consider a branch manager in a distribution business:

- A number of the costs are driven directly by the revenue level: the inventory required, the number of people needed to fill and deliver orders, and the cost of order processing.

- Sales with special characteristics represent a "derivatives of revenue" cost driver. Back orders drive some added purchasing and material processing costs. A marketing decision to stock a broad line of products adds to inventory, purchasing, and material processing costs.

- An example of an "outside requirements" driver is sales tax regulations, particularly if the branch sells in more than one state.

- Structural factors include location of customers and warehouses, and the number of warehouses from which the branch draws. These determine transportation, freight, and some personnel and telecommunications costs.

- Requests for service: Plumbing distributors, for example, maintain a showroom, at considerable cost, so that retailers can send their customers to see the products in a realistic setting before buying.

Procedures and processes, the way the work is done, is the second general class of cost drivers. Another way of saying this is that costs are driven by the choice of activities and inputs.

In general, the two biggest factors that affect procedure and process cost drivers are the degree of automation and the number of things an organization does versus what it buys. Regarding automation, increasing it makes costs more "fixed" relative to revenue. Compare the extremes of manual and automated factories. In automated factories the only labor costs are setup and maintenance of the machinery, while amortization of that machinery becomes a major cost. In manual factories, there is little of the latter, but large labor costs. The cost drivers thus are different. The number and types of products (i.e., the factory schedule, a derivative of revenue) are a major cost driver of the manual factory. In the automated factory the machines must be amortized independent of the factory load. Cost variation relative to number and types of outputs is limited to setup and perhaps maintenance costs. (We are assuming that raw material costs for given outputs are the same for both example factories.) Thus procedures and processes replaces revenue and its derivatives as the primary cost driver in automated factories.

"Buying" rather than "making" a particular item changes the activities involved in that item and the source of the input to subsequent activities. Labor costs should decrease, material costs should increase, and purchasing activities and costs change (from purchasing raw material and supplies to purchasing the finished item). If the "buy" decision is correct, overall costs should decrease. The costs of an item "made" are driven by raw material prices, the factory schedule, degree of automation, skill and wage levels, and possibly structural factors such as the proximity of workers to their inputs. The costs of things "bought" are driven mainly by the number required (analogous to the "factory schedule") and the price level.

The general price level is also a determinant of costs, and this includes the price levels for everything an organization buys: purchased material prices, wage levels, rent levels, and so on. This one is usually beyond the manager's control, and price changes can invalidate a budget quickly. Such price levels are always candidates for assumptions.

The recommended approach to the definition of cost drivers is threefold. First, concentrate only on the important cost drivers—those things that most strongly determine the organization's cost level. If monthly reports are an incidental cost, don't worry about what drives their costs. Second, progress from the definition of activities to the nature of the costs to the drivers of those costs. That is, rather than some general categories of cost drivers, look for what drives the individual cost elements: labor, purchased material, rent, utilities, etc. Third, where there is more than one way to describe a cost driver, choose the one that is closer to the organization. This facilitates thought processes leading to cost reductions. For example, a new product can be said to be driven by a "business decision" or by "competition." Choose "business decision," because that correctly reflects something that can be changed.

The entire process of determining costs and cost drivers is summarized in Figure 6-2.

Example: Planning an Organization's Work

To summarize the definition of an organization's work, as covered in Chapters 5 and 6, consider the example of a machine shop. The conclusions of the manager's analysis would be something like the following:

Primary Outputs: Machined parts of given types with given specifications

Figure 6-2. Determining the costs and cost drivers.

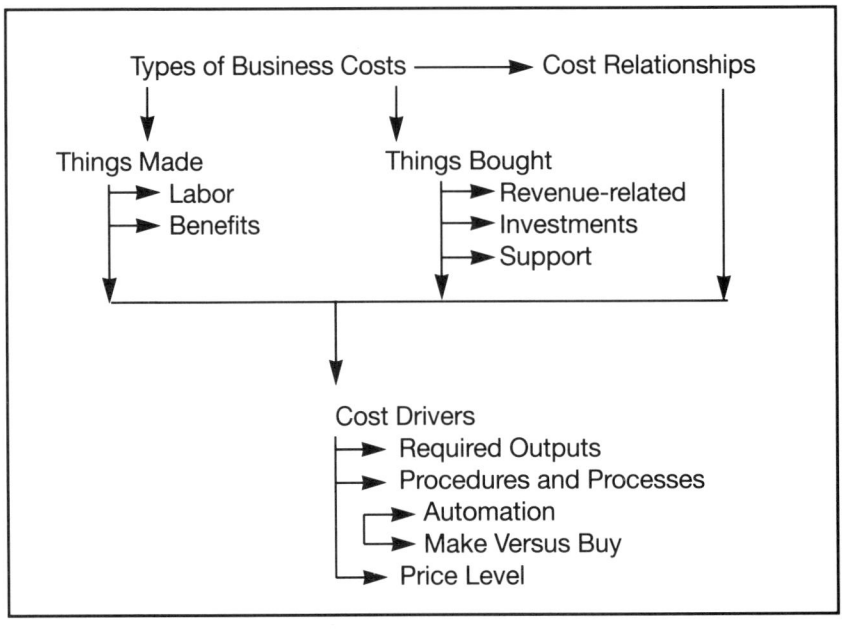

```
Types of Business Costs ─────► Cost Relationships
         │              │                │
         ▼              ▼                │
   Things Made     Things Bought         │
      ├─► Labor       ├─► Revenue-related│
      └─► Benefits    ├─► Investments    │
                      └─► Support        │
         │              │                │
         └──────┬───────┘                │
                ▼                        │
           Cost Drivers                  │
              ├─► Required Outputs
              ├─► Procedures and Processes
              ├─► Automation
              ├─► Make Versus Buy
              └─► Price Level
```

Understanding Costs and Cost Drivers 63

Information Outputs:	Reports on use and disposal of toxic materials
	Material requests (raw material and supplies)
	Budgets
	Monthly reports: output, quality, inventory, costs
Service Outputs:	Advice to engineering on design of machined parts
	Incidental advice and fabrication (management, customers, etc.)
Output Dictators:	Production plan
	Environmental regulations
	Budgeting and reporting requirements
	Incidental requests for machining
Activities:	Prepare material requests
	Receive material
	Maintain inventory
	Set up machines and material
	Machine material
	Inspect output
	Prepare budgets
	Prepare monthly reports
	Store, use, and dispose of toxic material
	Administer
Inputs:	Raw material
	Supplies
	Drawings and specifications
	Equipment
	Tools
	Training
	Instructions on use of equipment and tools
	Toxic material instructions
	Electricity and other utilities
	Financial numbers
Nature of Costs (deduced from the activities):	Labor
	Benefits

	Raw material
	Machining supplies
	Facility: rent, heat, light
	Electricity and other machining utilities
	Equipment (presumably capitalized)
	Tools (some possibly capitalized)
	Office supplies
Cost Relationships:	With fewer people there is more overtime.
	Buying partially worked raw material means less labor, electricity, and use of machinery; conversely, more machinery should mean cheaper raw material can be bought.
	More machinery (automation) means less labor.
Cost Drivers:	All the output dictators
	Type of machinery and automation level
	Work flow processes
	Location of suppliers
	Price levels for purchased items and labor

With this analysis in hand, the machine shop manager starts his budgeting by quantification of the outputs. He needs the actual or assumed production schedule, environmental reporting requirements, and management reporting requirements. From these he can forecast the level of activities that will be required in the next year and can start forecasting his people numbers and skills needs or surpluses, machinery needs, use of electricity and other utilities, etc. This leads to conclusions regarding whether his organization can produce the required outputs next year, and what the costs will be. Primary cost drivers are probably the production plan and the level of automation.

The detailed knowledge represented by such an analysis enables the manager to knowledgeably investigate at least four areas for performance/cost improvement:

1. Particular output parts requirements may result in abnormal costs and problems. Suggestions for redesign may improve costs and schedules with little or no product performance degradation.

Understanding Costs and Cost Drivers

2. New machinery may increase output or reduce labor costs for a given output, and improve schedules. The analysis plus the cost of the new machinery allows its payoff versus cost to be determined.

3. By considering individual output requirements (number and schedule) in detail, analysis of activities lets the manager suggest output schedule changes that will improve the machine shop efficiency. A simple computer model of machine shop activities—costs and schedules for different operations and parts—will facilitate this analysis (modeling is discussed in Chapter 9 and Appendix C).

4. For required activities for which the machine shop is not well suited, an intelligent tradeoff can be made between subcontracting and acquiring the needed machinery and skills.

All managers define and plan their organization's work to some extent; they could not function otherwise. The argument here is that it should be done deliberately, explicitly, and completely. There is no better way to prepare good budgets, defend them successfully, react to changes during the budgeting process, and react to problems and surprises through the year.

Tips and Traps

- Remember that acceptance of a product or service by a customer is a result; everything else is a cost. Management is paid to get results and minimize costs, all costs. The day is long past when the way to get ahead was to build a bigger organization. The way to get ahead now is to find ways to do things at lower cost. In fact, in these days of burgeoning employee lawsuits—for unlawful discharge, discrimination, sexual harassment, and surely grounds yet undiscovered—top management will be particularly pleased if you find ways to do more work without adding employees.

7
Dealing With Uncertainty: Assumptions

Figure 7-1. The planning work of budgeting.

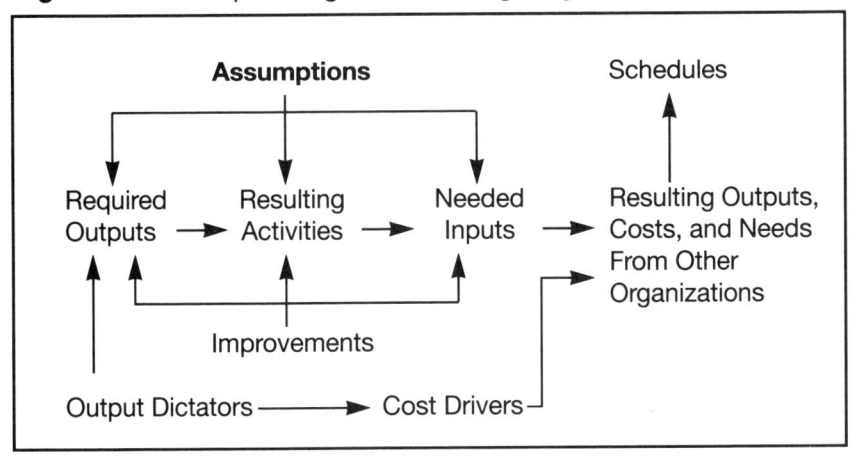

```
                    Assumptions                        Schedules
            ┌───────────┼───────────┐                      ▲
            ▼           ▼           ▼                      │
        Required    Resulting     Needed          Resulting Outputs,
        Outputs  →  Activities  →  Inputs    →    Costs, and Needs
           ▲  ▲        ▲            ▲              From Other
           │  │        │            │              Organizations
           │  └────Improvements─────┘
           │
        Output Dictators ─────→ Cost Drivers
```

The biggest cause of budgeting difficulties is that managers cannot know with confidence the amounts of required outputs and inputs for next year because of the uncertainty of the future and the uncontrollability of the outside environment. These problems cannot be avoided, but the intelligent use of assumptions is a powerful tool in overcoming their effects. (The place of assumptions in the work planning process is shown in Figure 7-1.)

Every company has important outside environmental factors (OEF), those outside factors that have significant impacts on the business but over which the company has no control or influence. Environmental regulations and price increases in important raw materials are examples. Similarly, all managers in the company, except top management, have internal uncontrollable factors (IUF), or those factors that arise from the strategy and management decisions made remotely from them. For a buyer in a retail company, a decision to shift emphasis from hard goods to soft goods is an example. Employee benefits costs are examples of both OEF and IUF for most managers, because some benefits costs are beyond the company's control and most managers have little influence on the benefits their companies provide.

The idea of the assumptions process is to (1) identify all important OEF and IUF that will affect the following year, (2) make the best assumptions possible about each of these OEF and IUF, (3) develop the budget numbers based on these assumptions, and (4) review these assumptions over the course of the year. In ENLIGHTENED, INC., if assumptions change during the year, the budget is changed. *The important result: Management is measured against what it can control and influence, and receives neither windfalls nor problems from events over which it has no control.* In MUDDLED, INC., the annual budget is inviolate, but managers can still communicate reality effectively to their superiors and peers through assumptions. They can thus make clear, for example, when bad results are caused by events that they cannot control, rather then poor performance.

Benefits From Explicit Assumptions

The following simple examples illustrate the advantages of assumptions as a budgeting tool.

- As a company-level example of an assumption for an outside environmental factor, consider a company that has a substantial subsidiary in Japan and does a large amount of business there. One of the important OEF is the yen-per-dollar relationship. Accounting rules require that the balance sheet be continually revalued in dollars. A balance sheet denominated in yen will be more or less valuable to the American parent, depending on whether the yen falls or rises against the dollar. This generates profits or losses completely outside the control of the company. This currency profit or loss can be significant. Thus it is appropriate to handle the yen-dollar relationship with a budgetary assumption regarding the average rate for the year in question. The budgeted currency profit or loss is then simply based on this assumption. Anytime during the year that there is a large move in the yen versus the dollar, or it is otherwise clear that the assumption will not hold, a new assumption will be made. If the company is ENLIGHTENED, INC., the budget will then be changed.

How is such an item handled without the assumptions process? To put the predicted profit and balance sheet of the Japanese subsidiary in the budget, someone must make an assumption about the yen-dollar rate for the coming year. Typically, however, this assumption is implicit and is not carried with the budget as it progresses to finalization. Currency profit or loss is then just part of the subsidiary profit budget that management is expected to meet.

If during the year the yen-dollar rate is quite different from the assumption (which is probable), management either gets a windfall or has a problem not of its own making. If the latter, there will be pressure to cut some planned, productive activity to get back on budget. In short, the company will be influenced to spend more or less—and management will be rewarded or punished—for an item or event that in the short term has no bearing on how well the company is performing. A good strategy may be crippled by cost cuts brought on totally by the action of this outside environmental factor.

- As an example of the use of an assumption for an internal uncontrollable factor, consider the manager responsible for publishing and distributing timetables in a commuter bus company. In the past, company bus schedules were stable and new timetables were published only twice a year. During the current year, however, for a variety of reasons, frequent and extensive schedule changes have required six new timetables. As a result, this manager's current year budget is in tatters. No one can tell her how many changes to expect next year; how should she budget? The answer is that she must assume something, deciding whether she thinks the new instability will continue or whether things will get back to normal. Chances are that she will be wrong, whichever way she goes.

If she announces the number of publishings as an assumption (e.g., "New timetables will be published twice during the year, in March and September"), at least two good things will happen. First, superiors will be made aware of an inherent uncertainty in her costs and be reminded of another cost that their decisions on schedule changes will affect. Second, attention and measurement will focus (at budget time and throughout the year) on her cost for a given amount of publishing. Minimizing cost per publishing, as well as ensuring accuracy and timeliness, is what she is paid to do—what she can control. She cannot control how much publishing she will be asked to do, and should not be measured on how well she guesses what that total amount will be.

Assumptions make management focus on important OEF, those that can sometimes control the company's destiny. They clarify the dependencies of one organization on another within the company. They make the budget more realistic; hidden pads in budgets are usually motivated by uncertainty about OEF and IUF. The psychological games will be reduced because the playing field changes from (*Boss*) "What can I talk you into?" and (*Subordinate*) "What can I get away with?" to (*both*) "Given the assumed conditions, what can *we* do, and what can *we* accomplish?" They make measurement more realistic and fair and make it safer to submit the "honest best" budget that top management and the stockholders want. Finally, they send an uplifting message to the organization that management will focus on, and distinguish among, factors under the organization's control and those not under its control.

The Assumptions Process

Figure 7-2 illustrates the assumptions process.

To be useful, assumptions must be specific and quantified and must represent a meaningful cause-and-effect relationship. The tendency is either to make assumptions that are too general to be useful (e.g., "The economy will not go into recession next year"), or so specific that they just assume that the manager's job will be done (e.g., "We will get budgeted new orders").

The key to getting useful assumptions is that they must relate

Figure 7-2. The assumptions process.

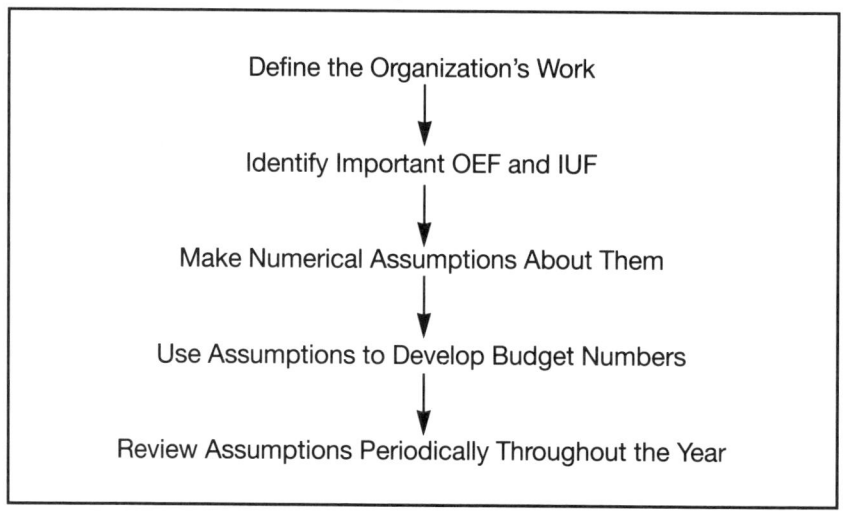

```
Define the Organization's Work
            ↓
Identify Important OEF and IUF
            ↓
Make Numerical Assumptions About Them
            ↓
Use Assumptions to Develop Budget Numbers
            ↓
Review Assumptions Periodically Throughout the Year
```

directly to both genuine OEF and IUF and to the organization's work. An assumption about the inflation rate is neither specific nor correlated enough to be useful. The inflation-related assumptions that an organization needs are about the specific, important elements that affect it: purchased material prices, entry wage rates, fuel costs, etc.

An example of an assumption that is not purely related to an outside environmental factor or internal uncontrollable factor is, for a purchasing manager, "We will keep material costs below 30 percent of sales." This statement combines at least the subjects of the type or mix of orders and sales, the price of purchased materials, and factory management factors such as shrinkage and rework. In other words, it just baldly assumes that the submitted budget number will be met.

Because it is difficult to get useful assumptions directly, the proper approach is to concentrate first on identifying the important OEF and IUF. If the definition of the organization's work has been done as explained in Chapters 5 and 6, the manager has in hand the nature of the organization's outputs, inputs, activities, output dictators, costs, and cost drivers. The task of identifying important uncontrollable factors is then simply to analyze the outputs and their dictators, inputs, and costs and their drivers to determine which important ones are uncertain and/or uncontrollable.

With the important uncontrollable factors in hand, the statement of assumptions is the straightforward choice of intelligent words and numbers that describe how each outside environmental factor and internal uncontrollable factor is expected to behave next year. The assumed numbers are then used in the budget, and other budget numbers are appropriately derived from them. The assumptions are prominently noted in budget submissions and reviews, and the reliance of all the budget numbers upon them is carefully explained.

Some assumptions should be given considerable time and effort, while others deserve very little. While the selected OEF and IUF and related assumptions should all be important for financial results, by definition, assumptions differ in importance from the point of view of management action. The yen-dollar rate in the earlier example was important financially, but surely no short-term action would result. Therefore, the magnitude of the assumption is not very important, and little time and effort should be spent on it.

On the other hand, assumptions regarding markets, competition, particular important customers, particular costs, and the like, are essential elements of management's plans. These must be the result of extensive thought and work and should be consistent with the judgments used in formulating company strategy and plans.

What If Assumptions Prove Incorrect?

How important is it that the budgeting assumptions turn out to be correct next year? The answer varies from assumption to assumption. It is important that assumptions that influence management action be reasonable, because the company is probably staking its future on the judgments that led to these assumptions. It is not important whether such things as the yen-dollar rate assumption are correct; the experts who forecast this relationship as part of their profession are often wrong, so why should we expect to be right?

But the question misses the point. The reason assumptions are used is that the budget must deal with future uncertainty about uncontrollable things. In the narrow sense of the budget for next year (as opposed to the broad sense of company direction and strategy for the long term), it is not important whether the assumptions are correct. The important thing is the thought about which important factors are uncontrollable, their articulation and communication, and the value of the assumptions in both managing and measuring.

The example of interest rates relative to a bank illustrates these points about the correctness of assumptions. The available interest rate spread between borrowing and lending can be crucial for a bank and is fundamental to lending strategy. However, the underlying rates themselves—the prime rate, Federal Reserve rates, etc.—are beyond the bank's control, and should be the subject of assumptions. It would seem important for the bank to make the correct assumption for next year on something so crucial. However, because interest rates are so inherently unpredictable, it would clearly be imprudent to base strategy in a way that "bets the bank" on a given interest rate prediction. The most important thing, then, is for the bank to react quickly to changes in interest rates, not to be right initially, which would be largely luck. Explicit assumptions allow an organization to continuously monitor the important OEF and IUF, and to be able to trace the effects of their changes through the budget, and the organization's work. Thus the value is not in the correctness of the initial assumption, but in the way the assumptions facilitate management in both focusing on things it can change and on reaction to surprises.

Choosing the Important OEF and IUF

To be useful in the budgeting process, the OEF must be quite specific and capable of quantification, and a relationship between their changes and organization results must be demonstrable. In identifying important OEF, one could start with general categories of outside uncontrollable factors that have important effects on the organization, such as the market, industry and competition, economy, government, and financial. However, this approach adds difficulty to the problem of tying identified factors to the organization. If the thought process started with "inflation," for example, you are forced to think of all the ways in which inflation may affect your organization.

While these general categories can be useful as background, the better approach is to start with the parameters that define the organization's work, mainly output dictators and cost drivers. This inside-out reasoning quickly identifies the specific OEF that are important to the organization. The machine shop example at the end of Chapter 6 showed the following output dictators and cost drivers:

Output Dictators: Production plan
Environmental regulations
Budgeting and reporting requirements
Incidental requests for machining

Cost Drivers: All the output dictators
Type of machinery and automation level
Work flow processes
Location of suppliers
Price levels for purchased items and labor

No more than inspection of these items is required to identify the OEF that are important to the machine shop: environmental regulations and price levels. Reasoning further, the manager might conclude that the most important price level is that for machining material. The conclusion, then, would be that assumptions are needed for machining material prices and changes in environmental regulations. These two items adequately define the effects of the uncertain and uncontrollable outside world upon the machine shop. The manager need not be concerned further with the economy, government, competition, etc.

In identifying the important IUF, there is another dimension of concern. Things dictated in other parts of the company are appropriate material for assumptions. However, plans and actions for the department in which the organization resides are things to which the manager is supposed to contribute. Assumptions are not appropriate for schedules, processes, and procedures by which the department gets its work done.

In the machine shop example, the manager is involved in "type of machinery and automation level," even though he cannot decide it by himself, so that item should not be the subject of an assumption. Neither should "location of suppliers," because the machine shop manager is involved in their choice. IUF appropriate for assumptions are "budgeting and reporting requirements" and "incidental requests for machining," although costs involved may be so small that assumptions are not needed. "Production plan" is a major determinant of cost, and much of it is beyond the machine shop manager's influence. However, the production plan directly describes machine shop outputs; if the budget is related clearly to that level of output, an assumption is not needed.

Thus, the machine shop manager may need only two assumptions: machining material prices and changes in environmental regulations. Although small in number, they are important, because large increases in either would have a large impact on next year's costs. (The machining material price assumption might be "Average cost of material will increase 10 percent over current year prices." If a small number of specific material items are particularly important, it would be better to make specific assumptions about each.)

The Assumptions Process at ENLIGHTENED, INC.

ENLIGHTENED designs assumptions into its budgeting process, from the beginning and at every level. The starting point is the identification of proper OEF. When the OEF are initially promulgated downward, all managers are expected to define their own IUF, as well as to recommend changes to the OEF list. The assumptions are then the best-known words and numbers associated with each outside environmental factor and internal uncontrollable factor, and they are directly inserted into the budget. Budget reviews at all levels then focus separately on the assumptions and on how the company should employ and deploy its resources.

As the budget year progresses, assumptions are reviewed and changed when a significant change in an outside environmental factor or internal uncontrollable factor occurs that invalidates an assumption. A key part of the process is that then the budget is changed as well. The point is continually and realistically to track, and react to, uncertainty, not to expect accuracy about the uncontrollables at least one year in advance. Directors and top management agree that businesses must operate in an environment of ever accelerating change. ENLIGHTENED uses the available information technology to let the budget track that change, rather than being maintained with inflexibility.

In the process the key role of final arbiter on when it is appropriate to change assumptions is held by the board of directors. The board, with its general experience and broad perspective, should be ideally suited to this role, and the integrity of the process requires that a disinterested body make these decisions. An important side benefit is that this deepens the involvement of the board of directors in the company's affairs in a particularly appropriate way, increasing the value of the board's contribution to the health of the company.

The Assumptions Process at MUDDLED, INC.

MUDDLED does not use an explicit assumptions process in budgeting. Assumptions are implicitly made by managers in generating numbers for their budgets. The process makes no deliberate distinction between what managers can and cannot control and influence.

In the absence of a company or division assumptions process, managers should conduct their own. They can do it alone, but, if their style and conditions permit, will get more benefit from involving their key people and bosses. The process should be inside-out. As part of the definition of the organization's work, identify the output dictators and cost drivers. Then decide which of these are important OEF and IUF. Make assumptions to cover these. State these assumptions prominently as part of the budget submission and in reviews, and relate the budgeted numbers to the assumptions.

The benefits, even in MUDDLED, INC., are considerable. Managers usually control so little of their destiny that they often feel that they are just reacting to events designed to complicate their lives. Some of that is unavoidable, but after going through the assumptions process, they reap the following benefits:

- Managers and their key people, and presumably the boss, understand their jobs better. By understanding what is controllable and uncontrollable, they are able to focus their energy on things that they can change.
- By thinking things through in this fashion, they can have the best budget possible under the circumstances.
- Knowing that the work will be subject to many changes throughout the year, managers now know what changes will have important effects on their functions, and to what they must react. They

can stay alert for the important changes and not get excited about changes that have minimal effect on their organization.

There remains the difficulty that managers can expect no budget relief from a changed assumption. In other words, while they recognize the subject of the assumption as an uncontrollable factor, MUDDLED's budgeting process does not so recognize it.

The antidotes for this difficulty will not remove it, but can reduce the problem. First, managers should communicate fully and carefully with their bosses and accounting. They should get them to understand what is uncontrollable, even if the budgeting process does not recognize it. Second, they should pad their budgets to allow for more negative manifestations of the OEF and IUF than they have assumed. Padding is not a recommended practice in an ideal world, but MUDDLED's budgeting process leaves them no choice. Assumptions, after all, are about uncontrollable things, and managers must protect themselves and their budgets.

Third, if their boss's style and personality allow it (i.e., if the psychology of budgeting is favorable), they should present everything factually and objectively, including the pads and their reasons. They want to influence the boss and peers to move toward better budgeting and the better management that will thereby result; they need a reputation for objectivity and honesty to do this successfully.

Tips and Traps

- The distinction between outside environmental factors and internal uncontrollable factors is important for thought and discussion because they are quite different things. However, that distinction is less important for a manager's budgeting; the important thing is that the uncontrollable factors be identified, regardless of whether they are OEF or IUF.

- Development, review, and discussion of budgeting assumptions provide an excellent vehicle for understanding critical factors for success. These are the relatively few factors, internal and external, that are crucial determinants of the organization's future. One hopes that every organization understands them, but they are sometimes difficult to articulate. The most important OEF will identify the external critical factors directly, while the IUF and related discussion of plans and assumptions will identify the internal critical factors.

8
Improving Performance: Gap Analysis

Figure 8-1. The planning work of budgeting.

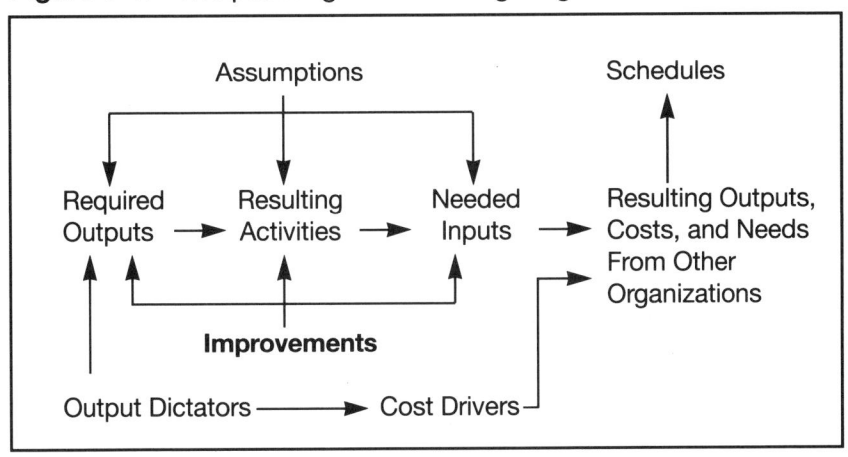

```
              Assumptions              Schedules
                  │                        ▲
      ┌───────────┼───────────┐            │
      ▼           ▼           ▼            │
  Required    Resulting    Needed    Resulting Outputs,
  Outputs  →  Activities → Inputs  →  Costs, and Needs
      ▲         ▲           ▲            From Other
      │         │           │            Organizations
      │      Improvements
      │
  Output Dictators ──────→ Cost Drivers
```

One important subject remains in our coverage of the planning work of budgeting. Managers are not paid to preserve the status quo; they are paid to improve the way things are done. (Improvements are highlighted in Figure 8-1.) All managers owe their employers continuous improvement and the best results possible in any situation, but the best results achievable never happen automatically. They must be known, planned, and managed. Since a manager's budget represents his or her plans for the next year, it should reflect this commitment to excellence and continuous improvement, and to "the best results achievable." However, as we saw in Chapter 3, all the inherent problems of budgeting (the conflict of objectives, measurement, the uncertainty of the future, the uncontrollability of the outside environment, and the psychological nature of budgeting) are arrayed against budgeting the best results achievable. It takes confident managers indeed to budget the best possible results when they know that they will be measured strongly on what they budget, that next year will be full of surprises (probably negative), and that their bosses will demand more, whatever they budget.

How do we resolve this conflict? We need a deliberate technique, as part of the planning work of budgeting, that lets managers:

- Define opportunities and problems in meaningful terms
- Relate proposed actions regarding these opportunities and problems to expected results
- Show the undesirable results of not carrying out the proposed actions
- Communicate all this clearly to bosses, peers, and subordinates

If these prescriptions can be met, managers can focus people's attention (in their organizations and in interacting organizations) and confidently work to improve performance and cost. The communication element of the prescriptions will protect managers from irrational attack on their plans, or at least make clear the adverse consequences of not following those plans. Most of all, perhaps, it will be made clear that demanded better results will not happen automatically.

The recommended technique that accomplishes these things is gap analysis.

Gap Analysis Defined

Gap analysis* begins with the identification of a parameter of concern and/or interest, called the *gap dimension*. This parameter can be anything from orders, sales, or profit to customer waiting times, proficiency in a particular skill, or factory rework levels. Two future projections of this parameter are then made: (1) the desired goal value and (2) the expected status quo result—i.e., of continuing to do the same things in the same way. These two projections define a gap, the difference between the goal and the expected status quo result. It is often useful to visualize and communicate this gap graphically (Figure 8-2). The all-important

---

*I am indebted to Michael Kami, an outstanding strategic management consultant, for introducing me to gap analysis some years ago. Further information on the subject is available in his book *Trigger Points* (New York: McGraw-Hill, 1988).

Improving Performance: Gap Analysis

Figure 8-2. Gap analysis.

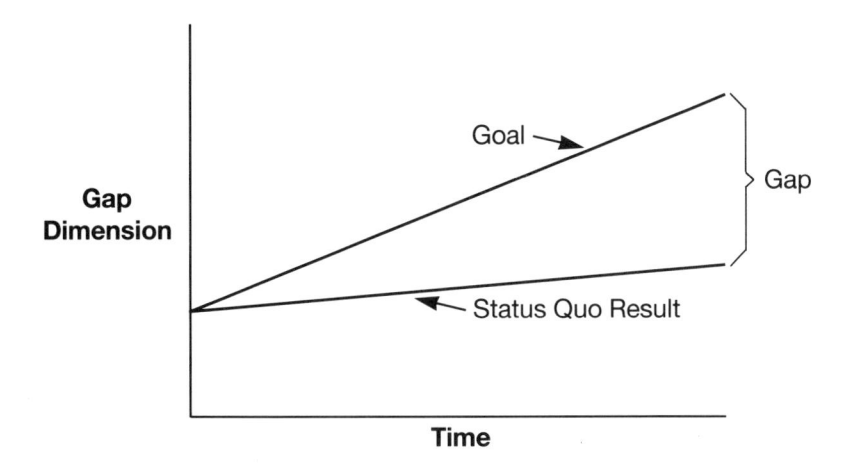

[Figure: A chart with "Gap Dimension" on the vertical axis and "Time" on the horizontal axis. Two lines diverge from a common origin: the upper line labeled "Goal" rises steeply, the lower line labeled "Status Quo Result" rises slightly. The vertical distance between them on the right is labeled "Gap".]

final step in gap analysis is then to develop action programs to fill the gap—i.e., to reach the desired goal.

To illustrate the concept, assume that a division general manager is committed to a goal of increasing profit 15 percent per year. The best available information convinces him that if the division keeps doing what it is doing profit will hardly grow at all. He has defined a gap between the goal of 15 percent profit growth and the expected status quo result of zero growth (Figure 8-3). This gap will not close by itself, but only by action on the part of the division. The definition of this gap gives him the means to state and communicate the problem to both superiors and subordinates, to begin the selection among alternatives, and to develop action programs to reach the goal.

In another dimension, assume that an accounting organization takes ten working days to close the books each month. For a number of reasons, no one is happy with that length of time, and the controller and her key people address the problem. In this case, the goal is not obvious, and requires some analysis and trade-offs. Ideally, everyone would want a one-day closing, but the goal must be possible, challenging but achievable. Assume that six days is chosen as an acceptable and practical goal. The gap dimension is closing time, the goal is six days, and the expected status quo result, if nothing is done differently, will continue to be ten days. The problem is thus defined. Alternatives such as new procedures, earlier cutoffs, and increased automation can be investigated. The goal and the gap focus the investigation, facilitate

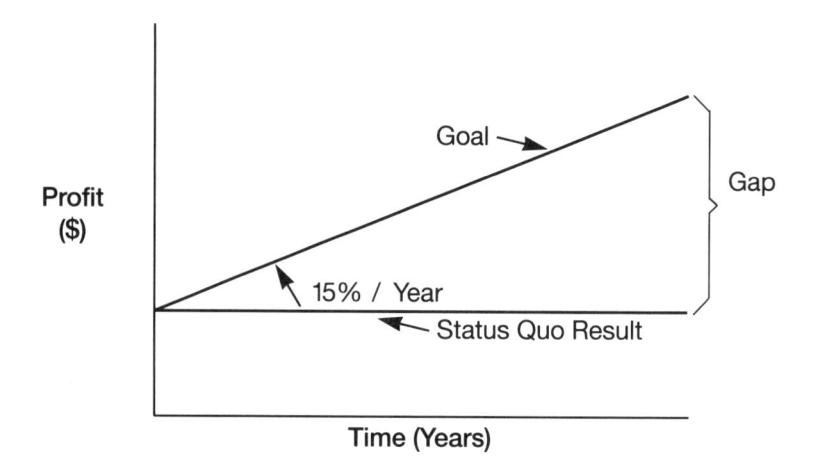

Figure 8-3. Division profit gap analysis.

```
Profit
 ($)
                    Goal
                                        Gap
          15% / Year
          ← Status Quo Result

              Time (Years)
```

communication, help the selection of the best alternatives, and drive the development and implementation of action programs to solve the problem.

Not all gaps can be filled. Original goals sometimes prove to be unrealistic, and must be lowered. Thus, an iterative process may be required between goals and actions until a realistic combination is developed.

Gap analysis is applicable at every level of a company and to almost all business parameters. The beauty of gap analysis lies in the many ways it can be applied, while giving all participants a common language in which to deal objectively with goals, problems, and actions. Specific, quantified gaps and related action programs will generate enthusiasm and focus the entire organization upon the pursuit of excellence. Gap analysis sends a message of a willingness to do the new and exciting things necessary to ensure the health of the organization in its ever changing environment.

An important benefit of gap analysis is a common language for communication. If planned actions and problems are communicated by means of specific gap dimensions, goals, status quo expectations, and resulting gaps, then misunderstandings will be minimized. Business needs and practices are usually sophisticated and their benefits abstract. The importance of a functional goal to the overall company results is often not obvious; similarly, the right functional goal to support overall company goals is also often not obvious. The language of gap analysis helps focus everyone on the right things.

Gap Analysis Applied to Budgeting

There are five steps in utilizing gap analysis in the budgeting process (see Figure 8-4).

1. *Select the gap dimensions.* For budgeting, the time horizon is specifically the next year. The process is begun by the selection of the parameters, or dimensions, for which the gaps are to be constructed. At the top levels of a company, the dimensions are commonly the most important financial parameters, such as profit. At lower levels, the dimension is often the most important output of the particular function: orders by the sales department, product performance by engineering, number of new hires by recruiting, etc. Many gap dimensions should result from particular problems on which a problem-solving focus is desired. Assume that a purchasing manager determines that her organization's main cost driver is simply the number of purchase orders. In that case, a gap analysis whose dimension is volume of purchase orders would be valuable.

The universe of potentially useful gap dimensions is huge. There

Figure 8-4. Gap analysis.

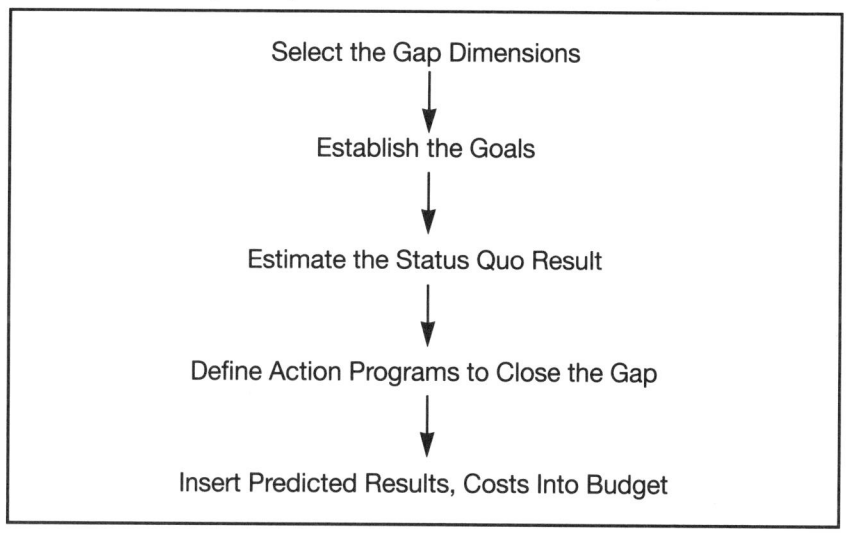

```
Select the Gap Dimensions
            ↓
    Establish the Goals
            ↓
  Estimate the Status Quo Result
            ↓
Define Action Programs to Close the Gap
            ↓
Insert Predicted Results, Costs Into Budget
```

are only two stringent requirements on their selection. The first is that the dimension must be something that pertinent managers can control, influence, and change directly by their actions. It would be useless for a customer service organization to do a gap analysis of profit, because profit is influenced by so many things about which customer service can do nothing. Second, any given organization should do only a small number of gap analyses. The purpose of gap analysis is to define, direct, and focus action. If many gaps are constructed, the result will be to defocus the organization as it tries to go in too many directions toward too many goals at once. Gap analysis should be reserved for the really important results and problems; often one or two gaps per organization is enough for any budget year.

2. *Establish the goals.* Selection of the goal(s) for the budget year for the chosen gap dimension(s) can be obvious and concurrent with the selection of the gap dimension, or it can require considerable analysis. If a company has a continuing objective of 15 percent profit growth per year, both the profit gap dimension and next year's goal are stated in the same breath on the first day of the process. On the other hand, considerable analysis of a problem is often required to set a proper goal for next year.

Goals used in the budgeting process must be realistic. If the gap dimensions are irrelevant, or if the goals are either too low or too high, meaningful improvement will not be achieved. Final goals must be specific, they must represent something that the organization can change through its actions, and they must be at the ambitious end of realism. Also, all goals must support and be consistent with company strategies and plans.

3. *Estimate the status quo result* expected for the budget year. Status quo means taking no new action to change results in the gap dimension. In other words, what is expected to happen if current methods and actions are continued? A common source of the status quo prediction is the recent trend modified by expected events and actions outside the gap dimension that will influence it.

4. *Define action programs to close the gap.* Good action programs are the direct result of the gap analysis, and the reason why it was done. Proper action programs are facilitated by the specificity and focus that the gap analysis provides. They are directed at specific results that can be measured, and are done by the people with the best knowledge and ability to attain those results.

5. *Insert predicted results into the budget.* If good gap analyses have been done, the development of the actual budget numbers is mechanical

and almost trivial. Ordinarily, the gap analysis goals (not status quo numbers) and the action resources required are the numbers that should be put in the budget. However, in MUDDLED, INC., the manager may wish to use the status quo result as the budget number, rather than the goal, depending on the particular psychological situation. If the goal was imposed by bosses, the budget number should probably be the goal. (In that case, the gap analysis supplies the means for the manager to explain what different things must be done, and what must happen externally, for the stated goal to be met.) If the gap analysis and goal were self-generated, managers may wish to protect themselves by putting the status quo result in the budget, leaving the goal as a private, beat-the-budget target.

Example: Choosing the Right Gap Dimension

Consider an investor relations function in a public company. The company in question has concluded that it will need to raise money within the next two years, and that some of it should be raised by selling stock. The company would therefore like to have a higher price for its common stock. The president and the board feel that the stock is undervalued, and investor relations is told to plan and budget a program for next year that will have a good effect on the stock price.

What is the proper gap dimension for investor relations? Emphatically not the stock price! Prices of common stock are influenced by many forces. The company's stock price may go up or down, independent of anything that investor relations does. Further, investor relations cannot turn bad news into good news. Such a gap dimension would give no information from which to plan investor relations actions.

However, it is generally accepted that "sponsorship" by important securities analysts helps maximize a stock price for given conditions; i.e., the more often respected analysts comment favorably on a stock, the more it will be bought. Therein lies a proper dimension for investor relations gap analysis: the number of important securities analysts who follow the company's stock. The status quo number one year later might be the same as the current number. A reasonable goal might be to double that number. The definition needs to be completed by stating what constitutes an "important" securities analyst (perhaps from a list of major research and brokerage firms), and what "follow the stock" means (e.g., mention in the analyst's written materials).

The first value of this gap analysis comes from the agreement between the president and the investor relations manager that this is the appropriate gap dimension relative to the needs of the president and the board of directors. It represents a deliberate decision that increasing the number of securities analysts is an appropriate investor relations focus for the next year.

The discussion involved will also reduce anyone's temptation to blame investor relations if the stock price goes down next year. There is a serious point behind this flippant statement: There is value in clarifying what superiors and subordinates believe an organization can change versus what it cannot.

Next, such a gap dimension provides a direct basis for an action program for investor relations. This might include more frequent contact and meetings with securities analysts, presentations by the president and the chief financial officer, additional news releases, background papers, and the like. The investor relations budget will follow directly from the action program. The budget will thus be tied to a program directed toward a specific goal, and both performance versus this goal and performance versus the budget will then be easily measurable.

Note that all this does not imply that the investor relations manager will be measured only on progress toward this gap analysis goal. Management is not that simple, and quality and quantity of output, the handling of crises, and general investor relations will all be part of the manager's appraisal. However, gap analysis provides focus about an important goal and direction for next year and communicates that focus to all concerned. Also note that multiple gap dimensions are possible. If this example company were particularly concerned also about poor stockholder relations, another gap analysis could be constructed to appropriately attack this problem. This would communicate a second focus for next year's efforts.

The final value of the example gap analysis is the major benefit in intramanagement communications. How to get a higher stock price is a fuzzy, controversial subject that engages the mind of every director as well as the top management group. The whole process from defining the gap dimension through to the action program and budget will focus and direct what could have been chaotic discussions. Gap analysis reduces fuzzy problems to specific dimensions that can be discussed and attacked.

Example: Gap Analysis and the Planning Work of Budgeting

To relate gap analysis to the planning work of budgeting, consider the purchasing manager in a company that sells and installs computer-communications network systems, broadly similar but each customized to customer needs. Quite a few of the elements of each system are bought, rather than made, by the company.

Assume that this purchasing manager has been told by her superior, in no uncertain terms but fortunately months before budgeting begins, that management is unhappy about the way purchasing's organizational costs have been increasing and that a cost cut will therefore be demanded in next year's budget. Also assume that increased competition has resulted in an increase in the number of customer proposals prepared, and this trend is expected to continue.

The purchasing manager involves her key people in a concentrated effort to analyze and define their organization's work. Purchasing's primary outputs are purchase orders to vendors, material cost estimates for customer proposals, and purchase order instructions to receiving and accounting. To keep the example simple, assume their analysis concludes that none of the information or service outputs are significant generators of activities or costs.

Purchasing's identified activities include evaluating vendors, maintaining the approved vendors' list, preparing purchase orders, negotiating purchase orders, expediting purchase orders, and providing material cost information for customer proposals. The principal inputs are material requests and bills of material for proposed systems.

The purchasing manager and her people conclude that their main cost drivers are simply the number of proposals and the number of material requests. The customer service function, particularly, generates a large number of small material requests, and each, by company instructions, requires extensive purchase order procedures.

Because the number of proposals is not expected to decrease, the people conclude that ways must be found to reduce the effort per proposal to keep total purchasing costs for proposals in line. They define a gap analysis whose gap dimension is the purchasing person-hours spent per proposal. As an ambitious and somewhat arbitrary goal, they pick a reduction of 30 percent from the status quo (current) hours. The goal, status quo, and resulting gap focus them on ways to cost proposed systems more efficiently.

As an example of a resulting action plan, assume that the current procedure has been to get vendor quotations on each sizable item in each proposal. Their analysis reveals many similarities from proposal to proposal, and relatively stable price structures. They conclude that if they can establish and periodically update a pricing database on many items, they can forgo the quotation activity for those items in proposals. An action plan for doing this is stated, responsibility assigned, and the work carried out.

Reducing purchasing proposal costs can be tackled within the purchasing organization, but the number of material requests is an example of a multifunction problem. Purchasing has no control over the number of material requests submitted, and they are required by company policy for practically all purchasing. The purchasing manager defines an interorganization gap analysis whose dimension is the number of material requests. She involves the organizations that are the main sources of material requests, and the people responsible for company control procedures. The status quo result for next year might be the recent trend: say, a 5 percent increase over this year. The goal is a specified reduction in that number. Again, the "task force" can then focus on specific causes and possible solutions to the costs resulting from the number of material requests. Action programs could include elimination of the need for a purchase order for items of less than a specified amount, less frequent and larger quantity ordering, process simplifications, etc.

If the purchasing manager can define her organization's work and conduct these two gap analyses before budgeting begins, she can confidently and realistically be responsive to the demand for lower purchasing costs next year. The cost reductions are based on real changes in the activities, the result of focused analysis by the people who best understand the requirements and the problems.

Advantages and Benefits of Gap Analysis

Here, then, are the advantages and benefits of gap analysis.

- *Gap analysis encourages the best performance possible,* by defining proper parameters, fostering ambitious goals for performance in those parameters, and promoting specific actions to meet the goals.
- *It has broad application.* It can be used in planning, budgeting, and the solution of particular problems. A particular gap analysis can be started by top management, by individual contributors, or by any management levels in between.
- *It provides a direct basis for action programs to satisfy goals and solve problems.*
- *It supplies a common language for communication among all levels* concerning the needs and problems of the company and its various organizations.

Improving Performance: Gap Analysis

- *It promotes agreement on important organizational parameters and goals.*
- *It clarifies what can be changed by management action, and what cannot.* As such, it is an answer to the old prayer "Lord, give me the courage to change what I can, the patience to accept what I cannot change, and the wisdom to know the difference."
- *It enables fairer measurement of managers* through this same clarification of things that managers can and cannot influence and change.
- *It yields valuable negative information*—e.g., that a particular goal is unreasonable, or that its satisfaction is improbable. This fosters focus on goals and activities that have a better chance for success.
- *It is a potent problem-solving tool.*

Tips and Traps

- The first obvious use of gap analysis is within a manager's own organization. Ordinarily, he or she should explain what is being done to the superior, and commit to meet the gap analysis goals. The more far-reaching application of gap analysis, if the environment allows it, is to propose and promote it for interfunction problems and/or performance improvement. Most companies have difficulty in solving multifunction problems. Gap analysis, particularly as part of budgeting, is a good way to do this.

- Each organization should do at least one gap analysis as part of budgeting. However, none should do very many, or else the result will be defocus and "milling around" instead of focus and improvement.

- In all aspects of budgeting, incremental benefits will result from incremental effort. It is never an all-or-nothing proposition. Busy managers should never conclude that improving their budgeting is too much work for this year. Improve one or more things this year, and others in subsequent years, experimenting and learning as you go. Improvements with the biggest payoffs are usually definition of activities, making proper assumptions, and gap analysis.

Part III
Generating the Numbers

9
Proper Budget Content

Figure 9-1. Generating the numbers.

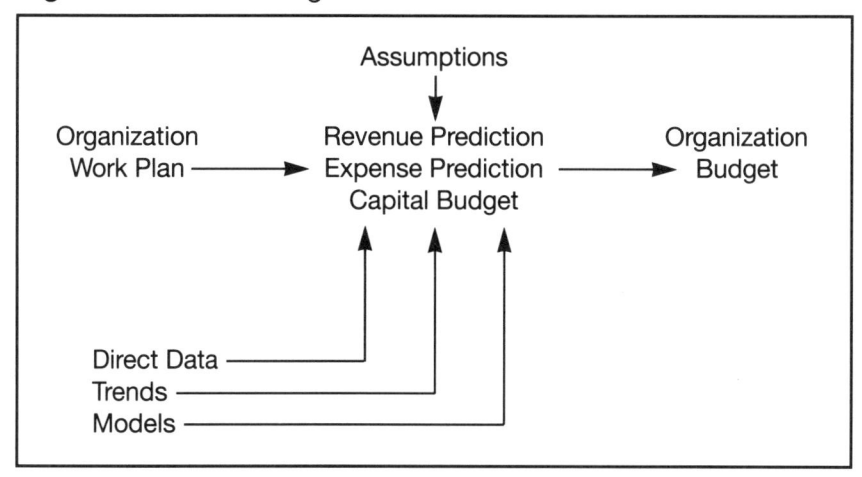

```
                          Assumptions
                              ↓
   Organization       Revenue Prediction      Organization
   Work Plan    ───→  Expense Prediction ───→    Budget
                       Capital Budget
                         ↑   ↑   ↑
   Direct Data ──────────┘   │   │
   Trends ───────────────────┘   │
   Models ───────────────────────┘
```

Good planning tells you how many products you have to make, how many sales calls you will make, or how many loan officers you will use to try to make a given number of loans. However, you still must numerically predict the revenue, expense, and capital expenditures that will result from these planned actions.

The problem, again, is the ever present uncertainty of the future. The numbers that express expected performance next year are necessarily estimates. For good budgeting, these estimates or predictions must be as probable and meaningful as they can.

The proper generation of budget numbers is the subject of Part III as a whole (see Figure 9-1). This chapter treats the subject in general, discussing the sources of numerical prediction and their use. Succeeding chapters discuss the three types of numerical prediction involved in budgeting: revenue, costs, and capital expenditures.

Sources of Budget Numbers

There are only three sources of numerical predictions for budgeting: direct data, trends, and models. Direct data means information that directly yields numerical values of budget parameters. Sales backlog (orders received but not yet sold) to be shipped next year is an example; these are specific sales that you can predict with confidence. Trends are the general direction in which particular parameters have been moving; extrapolation of trends into the future is the way they are used in budgeting. If a particular product had sales of 40, 80, and 120 units respectively in the last three years, the trend would say that 160 units would be sold next year. Models (strictly mathematical models) are equations or sets of equations that describe the relationship among parameters. The equation

$$\text{Profit} = \text{Sales} - \text{Expense}$$

is a model, although too simple to be of much value in a budget. For given values of sales and expense, this model tells us what the profit will be.

(Assumptions—Chapter 7—used for uncontrollable factors and for unknown data in the early stages of budgeting, could be called a fourth source of budget numbers. However, they are used to replace data or as model inputs, so we prefer not to consider them separately, but rather in conjunction with direct data, trends, and models.)

All three of these sources of budget numbers use "data," of course, meaning known, quantitative information. The distinction is in the way the data are used. "Direct data" means that the data themselves are sufficient to enter into the budget (e.g., revenue from backlog). Use of "trends" means that past and present data must be analyzed to discern the expected values for next year (e.g., next year's cost for something whose cost has been increasing every year). Use of "models" means that available data are combined in calculations to get the needed parameter value (e.g., assembly costs of a new product, calculated from a definition of operations involved and data on similar operations).

The problems, then, that cause poor budgets, even if good planning work was done, are misuse of direct data, trends, and models in generating the budget numbers. Their proper use will be discussed in the following sections.

Direct Data

Direct data are the best source of numerical predictions for the budget, provided that they are valid and used appropriately. Direct data are values of budget entries that are substantiated by specific knowledge and information. Therefore, these values can be used with high confidence. If you are required to predict the costs of fifty units of a given product, and all the material for those products is already in inventory (i.e., bought and paid for), you know what the material costs of building those fifty units will be.

Examples of parameters for which direct data can often be used in budgeting are:

- Rent
- Salaries of personnel
- Costs of a mature product
- Costs of purchases that have firm quotations
- Costs of doing things that have been done before
- Interest income from fixed investments

Direct data do not have to be certain to be the best source of a budget number. Change the example of having to predict the material costs for building fifty units of a given product to one in which the material must be bought rather than just retrieved from inventory. Now you cannot be certain of the material costs. In general, such material prices are an uncontrollable outside factor, appropriate for an assumption if large enough to be important. However, let's assume you know the vendors and have reason to trust what they tell you. If they say prices will stay the same, you still have direct data: known current prices plus vendors' statements. You cannot be certain about material costs in this case, but direct data are still the best source of the budget number.

The most common misuse of direct data is stretching it beyond the time when it is meaningful. Again consider the same material costs for fifty units, but now assume that purchase prices for these materials are unstable and you do not know the vendor. You still have data on current material costs for the product, but those data are not reliable for next year. In this case, trends cannot help. You must make an assumption for next year's value based on the best analysis you can make of the situation. You are then using an assumption based on a model (or "model-type thinking"), rather than the data that you have on this year's prices. In general, past and current data should not be directly used when uncontrollable outside factors are involved.

Another example of stretching data is the way some people labor to put specific customer names and dates on orders expected during the fourth quarter of next year. Assume that the company in question relies upon a few, large orders. If the order cycle (from initial expression of interest to signing the order) is usually six months, you cannot possibly know the specific identity of customers who will place orders a year from now. Attempting to be so specific implies knowledge that you do not have, and the predictions will undoubtedly be wrong. Rather than trying to use direct data, it would be more accurate to predict fourth-quarter orders from trends or a model involving such things as market size, known prospects, and number of sales calls.

You are indeed fortunate if you can completely fill out your budget forms with direct data. This is the exception rather than the rule. The inherent uncertainties cause most budget numbers properly to be generated from trends and models.

Trends

"Trends" mean the direction in which something has been moving. If a particular cost is $100,000 one year, $120,000 the next, and $140,000 the next, a trend has been established of an increase of $20,000 per year. Learning curves in a factory or any repetitive operation are examples of the use of trends; it is expected that people will complete tasks faster, and thus cheaper, as they become more experienced in doing them.

Seasonal trends are also a source of budget information. Toy and ice-cream businesses have obvious seasonable characteristics; many other businesses have seasonal variations just as valid. Since performance against the budget is reviewed and measured monthly, seasonal characteristics must be correctly reflected.

The more data points there are, the more valid is the trend established from those data points. There are various sophisticated ways to determine trends, using the principles of statistics and regression analysis. Such precision is generally not necessary in budgeting; it is sufficient to estimate a trend by averaging or by plotting the points and visually fitting a straight or curved line to them. If purchase prices for certain material have increased 4 percent, 7 percent, 6 percent, 3 percent, and 7 percent in each of the last five years, it would be reasonable to say that the trend is a 5–5.5 percent increase per year. If those same prices increased 2 percent, 5 percent, 4 percent, 7 percent, and 8 percent, there is a trend of accelerating increases, and one would say that the trend predicts about a 10 percent increase next year. Since we are dealing with uncertainty, there is no value in doing the work required to define that trend precisely to a thousandth of a percent.

The use of trends to generate budget numbers carries an implicit assumption that the trend will continue. Therein lies the problem. Few trends of any kind last six years, as in the above examples; the world changes too fast for conditions that defined the trend to stay the same. More than that, however, the formation of any trend carries no guarantee that it will continue if changing conditions and uncontrollable factors are at work. Witness the stock market, which often seems to invalidate a trend almost as soon as there are enough data for it to be recognized.

The most common misuse of trends is the blind following of them. If widgets have been assembled by the company for two years and the process has not been changed, the cost of assembling a widget next year is very predictable from the trend of past and current costs. However, one can never say that an orders trend will continue without examining market factors, competitors' actions, the general economy, etc. If a deep recession suddenly arrives, a luxury-car dealer should certainly not predict a sales increase next year just because there were increases last year and this year.

The opposite is also a common source of the misuse of trends: ignoring them without a good reason. If sales of widgets have been flat for two years and nothing in the product or market has changed, a sales manager who predicts doubling of widget sales next year clearly has some explaining to do.

The proper way to use trends in budgeting is always as questioned trends. If the number predicted by the trend is to be used in the budget, a deliberate conclusion must have been reached that the trend will continue. Orders and revenue trends are always suspicious. Cost trends are more reliable, but purchase prices are also uncontrollable, and management actions to change the way things are done invalidate trends. Seasonal trends are also subject to change if certain market characteristics change or if the market puts the products in question to different uses.

The converse is also true: There must be a reason for ignoring a trend. The trend must have been questioned and a deliberate conclusion reached that the trend is no longer valid.

Models

Modeling is another major subject, a professional specialty. Our concern is not modeling in general but the application of models to the problem of generating numbers for budgets.

Models are relationships among parameters expressed in equation form. They are built with information, knowledge, or assumptions about elements of a total parameter of interest. That is, they are built with partial data. Their use is not as difficult as it may seem; simple models are generally all that is needed for budgeting. In fact, all managers already use models in their budgeting, whether they recognize it or not. The following simple thought process is an example of modeling: If I know the cost of doing something once and there are no economies of scale involved, the cost of doing it ten times is simply ten times that unit cost.

Thus models can be implicit, but are being used nonetheless. Assume that a sales manager says, "There are 1,000 customers for this product and they generally replace their equipment every five years, so I believe that there will be 200 orders next year." That sales manager has built this implicit model in his mind, even if the equation is never written down:

$$\text{Next Year's Orders} = \text{Market} / 5$$

Modeling is second nature to some managers, particularly in this computer-literate age, but is unfamiliar territory for some. Appendix C, Use of Personal Computers in Budgeting, discusses modeling as one of the computer applications. Here we illustrate modeling with an example of the usefulness of an organization cost model to a manager, using a machine shop example similar to that developed in Chapter 6:

The simplest cost model for an organization expresses total cost as the sum of its various elements:

$$\text{Total Cost} = \text{Labor} + \text{Material} + (\text{Etc.})$$

The next steps are to divide these gross cost categories into useful elements, and to relate them to outputs. For a machine shop, it may be most useful to express costs as

$$\text{Total Costs} = \text{Machining Costs} + \text{Overhead}$$

Overhead includes administration, heat, light, office supplies, and depreciation—i.e., the "fixed costs."

The machining, or "variable," costs can then be expressed as the summation of the costs of the activities of each machine, per eight-hour day:

$$\text{Machine Cost} = \text{Labor} + \text{Material} + \text{Electricity}$$
$$\text{Labor} = \text{Labor Rate} \times (\text{Setup Time} + \text{Operating Time})$$

Labor operating time can then be expressed in terms of times per unit and the number of units for different products. Setup time is the number of product changes per day and the setup times for each product.

For each product,

$$\text{Material} = \text{Material per Unit} \times \text{Number of Units}$$
$$\text{Electricity} = \text{Rate} \times \text{Time per Unit} \times \text{Number of Units}$$

These two expressions are then summed over the different products to be made.

Putting these last four equations together relates the cost of one machine per day to the numbers and types of products done on the machine.

$$\text{Machine Cost} = \text{Labor Rate} \times (\text{Setup Time} + \text{Operating Time}) + \text{Material per Unit} \times \text{Number of Units} + \text{Electrical Rate} \times \text{Time per Unit} \times \text{Number of Units}$$

Summing this cost for each machine yields total machining costs, and thus the total cost of the machine shop, for a given quantity and mix of output:

$$\text{Total Cost} = \text{Sum of Each Machine Cost} + \text{Overhead}$$

With the production schedule, this can be extended into weeks, months, and the entire year.

The resulting cost model is complex for a machine shop of any size and variety of output, but easily handled on a personal computer spreadsheet. With this model, the machine shop manager can:

- Quickly predict budget costs for a given mix and quantity of output
- For that mix and quantity, determine if personnel and machines, or overtime, must be added
- Conversely, see if layoffs are needed and/or idle machines can be expected
- Do "what if" analyses to see if loading, schedule, or process changes can improve output versus cost
- Quickly replan if budget requirements change, or when the real world turns out to be different from the budget during the year

How are models used in budgeting? Models *must* be used when no valid data or trends exist for a number that must be generated. Predicted numbers for new activities must come at least partially from models, either explicit or implicit. New activities, products, and projects must be predicted from models, because data and trends do not exist. Even for mature activities, models must be used beyond the time in which data or trends are valid. Finally, models must be used, along with trends, when data are not meaningful to a particular business.

Models *should* be used as a supplement and a reasonableness check for data and trends.

Models *can* be used as a powerful aid to the planning work of budgeting. Consider an engineering manager who has put project manpower planning onto a personal computer spreadsheet. (This is an example of a model that expresses variables versus time in a table rather than in equation form.) Before the budgeting process begins, she can lay out the spreadsheet for next year, with months (or weeks, if necessary) across the top and already assigned projects in the first field down the left side. From project plans, she can then put in personnel assignments to the different projects by names and by week or month. (Input the names in such a way—e.g., in the second field—that a sorting by name can yield total assignments for each person.)

The spreadsheet gives the manager a head start on next year's budget by showing her how many new projects are needed or can be handled and skills and numbers of people in short supply or oversupply. By doing it ahead of time, she can perhaps influence the project planning for next year. When the sales and product development budget requirements arrive, the manager has a tool already available to determine capacity versus the planned workload. She will be able to suggest schedule changes that can smooth peaks and valleys, to understand hiring or layoff requirements, and to budget costs quickly.

Misuse of models results from poor or invalid modeling (for which prior definition of the work plus knowledge and intelligence are the main antidotes), but most of all from their insufficient use. MUDDLED, INC. is not fluent in modeling, and top management demands to see data or trends for everything, whether valid or not.

When and How to Use the Different Sources of Numbers

The use of direct data, trends, and models is treated further in the prediction of revenue, costs, and capital expenditures in the next three chapters. To close this chapter, we summarize the key points about their general use (Figure 9-2):

Figure 9-2. Proper use of budget number sources.

> *Direct Data:* Always, if available and *valid*
>
> *Trends:* Never ignore, but always question
>
> *Models:* When valid data or trends do not exist

- Direct data should always be used when available and valid for the particular application.
- Trends should never be ignored, but they should always be questioned before use. If the trends involve uncontrollable factors, these should be treated with assumptions.
- Models are used because in many situations they are the most accurate source of predictions in the uncertain world, and because their use does not mislead in the same way that use of invalid data or trends does.

There is no way to take the uncertainty out of the future. Stretching data, extrapolating invalid trends, or carrying numbers out to five significant digits do not help; they only create a harmful illusion. The right way to deal with the uncertainty of the future is to recognize it, plan the work intelligently, make assumptions for the important factors which are uncertain and uncontrollable, and use the best available source for the actual budget numbers.

Tips and Traps

- While ignoring valid trends is less of a problem in most companies than the blind following of trends, it probably takes up more time in budget reviews. This is because it is easier for a superior to see that managers are not following trends than to understand that a trend is invalid. Be particularly prepared to justify your conclusion to disregard an established trend.

- If, as in MUDDLED, INC., your superiors demand that data be reflected in every budget entry, you must supply what they request. If caught in such a situation, use models yourself and judiciously explain your budget in terms of your models, always seeking greater acceptance for that better source of some budget numbers.

10

Revenue Forecasting

Figure 10-1. Generating the numbers.

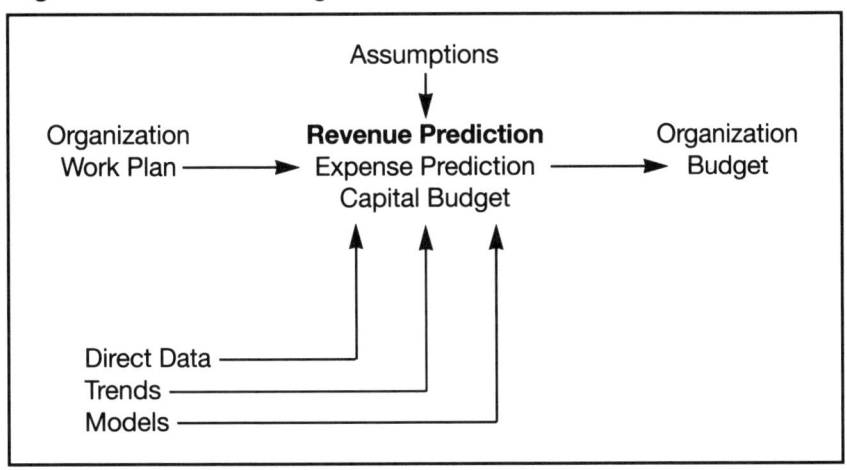

```
                          Assumptions
                              |
                              v
  Organization          Revenue Prediction        Organization
  Work Plan    ----->   Expense Prediction  ----> Budget
                        Capital Budget
                         ^   ^   ^
                         |   |   |
  Direct Data -----------|   |   |
  Trends --------------------|   |
  Models ------------------------|
```

Revenue forecasting represents the greatest level of "uncertain planning" in budgeting, and it is both the most critical and the most difficult task. It is the most critical because the entire budget flows from it. The amount and type of revenue expected is the most fundamental driver of the whole company's activities, and therefore its costs. It is the most difficult task because of the uncertainty of the future, and the fact that there are always things about orders and sales that are uncontrollable. Revenue prediction is highlighted in Figure 10-1.

Revenue Drivers

The proper starting point for forecasting revenue is to consider what drives it. There are six general revenue drivers from which the models and important factors for a given business can be identified:

1. *The relevant market.* This includes its overall size, how many will buy in a year, seasonal tendencies, and the like. A supercomputer maker needs to know its total market specifically, probably even the actual names of all the laboratories, agencies, and businesses that are potential supercomputer users. A luxury new-car dealer knows his market in terms of statistics: the number of people in the trading area with annual incomes exceeding a given amount, for example. Each company has particular market parameters within the market that are of direct interest.

2. *The state of the relevant economy.* For the supercomputer maker, the size of the research and development portion of the defense budget is probably more pertinent than the state of the general economy, although the entire world economy may be pertinent to such a business. The new-car dealer, on the other hand, is primarily concerned only with the state of the local economy.

3. *The actions of competitors.* These include new products, price changes, entries and exits, and the like. This is probably both the most important driver and the one that often gets slighted in the budgeting process. Budgeters particularly tend to underestimate the *reactions* of competitors to new company marketing tactics.

4. *The maturity of the business's products and services.* Sales of new products are more difficult to predict than those of mature products, but successful new products grow rapidly. Mature products cannot grow much, and will eventually decay, unless deliberately revitalized by new features or new applications.

5. *The sales and marketing effort.* Depending on the type of business, this can primarily be the sales force—its size, coverage, efficiency, and effectiveness—or primarily the marketing activity—the amount and effectiveness of advertising, the design of the product versus the competition, sales promotion, and the like.

6. *Capacity.* Although listed last, the importance of capacity as a revenue driver should not be underestimated. Orders and customers will not become revenue unless the desired product or service can be generated and delivered. Capacity here should be viewed in the broad sense to include skill and capability as well as time and amount of resources.

Note that, of the six generalized revenue drivers, only the last three, maturity of products, sales and marketing, and capacity are within the company's control. The other three are uncontrollable outside environmental factors (OEF), and are candidates for important budgeting assumptions, as discussed in Chapter 7. It is necessary to study the expected outside environment, and to make assumptions about it, before predicting orders and sales. Thus one starting point for budgeting orders and sales is identically the assumptions process explained in Chapter 7. (The three drivers that are controllable by the company may not be within the control of the manager who is budgeting revenue. However, they are generally not appropriate for assumptions because that manager is part of the organizational team responsible for determining them, as explained in the discussion of internal uncontrollable factors (IUF) in Chapter 7.)

Orders and Revenue Assumptions

Assumptions related to orders and revenue are usually controversial. Any manager responsible for budgeting revenue should use assumptions, by all means. Proper assumptions focus management on both the things that it can change and the uncontrollable things it must watch for surprises, and foster fairer measurement and better management. But they should be used carefully. Any assumption which seems to be an excuse for less than energetic salesmanship will be greeted skeptically.

The best candidates for revenue assumptions are the orders/sales drivers and special factors in the particular situation. Make the subject of the assumption something that is clearly uncontrollable and beyond your influence. The financial health of a major customer is clearly beyond your control. If that customer accounts for 40 percent of your revenue and you believe that percentage will reduce by half next year because of the customer's financial difficulties, you are making both an appropriate and probably acceptable assumption. Further, the assumption will alert management and the whole organization to a problem.

Some candidates for assumptions that are both appropriate and usually acceptable are the following:

- Business conditions and financial ill health of major customers (such as a bankruptcy)
- Relevant economic conditions, but they must be specific (the local effect of closure of a nearby military base)
- The short-term effects of unusual actions of competitors ("buying" market share with obviously low prices)

- Policy decisions by customers that affect your business with them (a decision to "make" something previously bought from you)
- New government regulations that affect the use of your product (new waste-handling requirements)

On the other hand, any assumptions regarding new products are usually inappropriate. Everything about a new product is a judgment and is uncertain. Related assumptions will make you appear to be trying to back away from a responsibility and a commitment.

The process for generating assumptions is as explained in Chapter 7: inside-out reasoning. Define first the things that have important effects on the level of revenue, and then see which of those are uncontrollable and thus assumption candidates.

Forecasting Prices

Revenue forecasting includes pricing because revenue is budgeted in dollars, not units or amount of customer traffic in a store. The way prices are determined and used varies widely, determined by the industry, the market, and company policy. Large contract businesses usually depend on quotations and negotiated prices. Various product businesses use a bewildering array of price lists and discounts. Some sell only at a fixed price determined by management, while others change prices every day. Some product and service prices are based on value, and others on cost.

For the narrow purpose of budgeting, managers need to predict only what next year's prices will be, not the theory or philosophy behind their company's pricing policies. In developing revenue budgets, the best way to approach pricing is (1) as an integral part of the revenue prediction process, plus (2) as a subject about which you must learn the pertinent company policies, and industry practices (from bosses, marketing and sales management, and finance).

In general, prices are driven by the same revenue drivers discussed previously: relevant market, relevant economy, competition, product maturity, sales and marketing effort, and capacity. The key to predicting prices is, again, to make proper use of all available direct data, trends, and models. A quotation to an orders prospect is direct data, but judgment must be applied to determine how much the quoted price will be reduced in negotiations. Similarly, current prices are direct data, but trends, model relationships, and outside factors must be analyzed to determine if current prices should be used. Price trends must be analyzed for factors that might invalidate them before being used. Pricing models are particularly useful for maturing products in some industries. Financial models involving inflation, cost of money, currency rates, etc., are useful at times. (Inflation models became second nature to people in budgeting in the 1970s and early 1980s, just about the time when inflation decreased rapidly. The general feeling in 1980 was that high inflation was a trend which would last forever.)

Different Types of Businesses Relative to Revenue Budgeting

Unfortunately for a general discussion, revenue budgeting varies greatly across different types of businesses. Before discussing a process, we must note the main types.

The first dividing characteristic is the concept of "orders." An order is an agreement to buy something at a specified future time and price, and implies that work must be done before delivery. Orders are a meaningful and important concept for manufacturing, some distribution, and some service and project businesses. However, they mean nothing for any business in which the customers just come through the door and buy something. The latter include most retail businesses and just about every cash business.

Even when the customer "orders" something, but the order is filled within a week or two, the concept of orders is not meaningful to budgeting. Orders are "meaningful" only when they are useful in planning future revenue. One or two weeks is "current" rather than "future" in the budgeting sense.

Where orders are meaningful, direct data can be used in revenue budgeting. "Backlog" (i.e., orders received but not yet delivered, or "sold") is confident direct data about revenue expected next year. Also, if orders are meaningful, good orders prospects can be inserted as direct data revenue forecasts, provided the data are not "stretched" beyond their usefulness.

The revenue budgeting problem is also quite different for the few-but-large sales business and the many-but-small sales business. Call these "hockey" and "basketball" businesses. In hockey games (businesses), sometimes the team does everything right but the goalie knocks the puck aside and no goal (order and sale) is scored. However, one needs very few goals to win the game (achieve good revenue). Conversely, in basketball games (businesses), no single basket (order/sale) is very important, but one has to get a large number of them to win.

In the computer business, a supercomputer manufacturer is an example of the former while a personal-computer maker is an example of the latter. Most retail companies are basketball businesses, although new-car sales in a luxury car dealership is probably a hockey business. Other examples of hockey businesses are military systems contractors, airplane manufacturers, and mergers and acquisitions in corporate finance. Basketball businesses include small-appliance manufacturers, consumer banking, and life insurance.

For revenue budgeting in a basketball business, you can use probabilities, statistics, and experience to relate orders, where applicable, and revenue to marketing and sales effort. Data and trends on orders per sales call or revenue per advertising dollar, for example, can be developed into model relationships that let you predict orders and revenue based on sales and advertising expense. You have no way of predicting individual orders or sales, but you do not care because an individual event is not important.

In a hockey business, each order and sale is quite important, and the presence or absence of just one particular order can make or break the year. In that case, little value can be obtained from the probability, statistics, and effort relationships on which the basketball business relies. Emphasis must be on analysis and forecasting regarding a relatively small number of individual prospective customers.

Generating the Revenue Numbers

Having divided businesses into these fundamental types—according to whether orders are meaningful to them or not, whether they are hockey or basketball—we can describe the recommended six-step generic process and note the way it differs among the different types (see Figure 10-2):

1. *Identify the factors that determine and drive revenue* for the specific budgeting situation. For the basketball business, these are specific applications of the general revenue drivers: the relevant market, the relevant economy, competition, maturity of products, marketing and sales effort and priorities, and capacity. In addition, the hockey business must analyze its market, almost by name, as well as the growth or decay of that market and its position in the market.

2. *Develop a model* of the most important parameters and relationships that will determine next year's revenue level. The hockey model

Revenue Forecasting

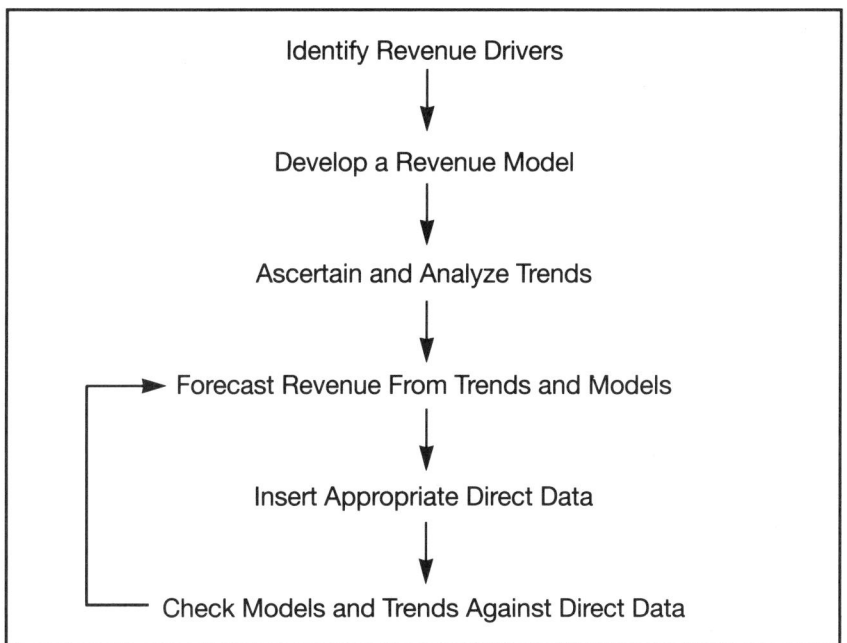

Figure 10-2. Revenue budgeting.

```
            Identify Revenue Drivers
                      ↓
           Develop a Revenue Model
                      ↓
           Ascertain and Analyze Trends
                      ↓
      ┌──► Forecast Revenue From Trends and Models
      │               ↓
      │    Insert Appropriate Direct Data
      │               ↓
      └──  Check Models and Trends Against Direct Data
```

must deal with small numbers of customers, while the basketball case will include more-general relationships developed from experience. (This step is a major activity only once, thereafter needing only possible updates for changes.)

3. *Ascertain the relevant trends,* both for revenue and for the revenue drivers. Then *analyze the trends* to determine whether they will hold or be changed by particular outside factors or company actions (such as new products or increased advertising). Trends have major application in the basketball case, but are of limited use in the hockey business.

4. *Forecast next year's revenue from the appropriate combination of trends and models.* This involves estimating the values of important factors, for insertion into the model and for analysis of trend validity. Assumptions should be included for important factors whose values for next year are unknown and uncontrollable. Again, the hockey model will be more oriented toward individual potential customers.

5. *Insert direct data where appropriate.* This is usually only pertinent to situations in which orders are meaningful. It is much more important

in the hockey case; in fact, direct data are the only valid budget entries within the order cycle time.

6. *Finally, check models and trends against available direct data,* such as backlog and good orders prospects. Again, this is more useful in the hockey case, because direct data are more important there. If the models or trends do not fit the direct data, they must be reevaluated and questioned.

When the hockey and basketball cases for revenue budgeting are compared, the former is found to be more difficult because individual orders and sales are so much more important. As a small compensation, the hockey business can use direct data whereas the other cannot. However, this is a mixed blessing because there is always a tendency to stretch direct data to the point of misuse.

Forecasting of Major Orders

An important question for businesses in which orders are a meaningful concept is: *Which orders predictions should come from direct data and which from questioned trends and models?* The key is the minimum time ordinarily involved from the identification of a prospect until the order is closed. Whatever time is thus included into the next year must be covered by direct data: identified potential customers already in the order cycle. If it ordinarily takes at least eight months from first contact to closing of the order and the budget is being prepared in early November, the first six months of the next year must be budgeted from data on known, confident prospects. In other words, in November all the possible prospects are known for orders before July of the following year. Neither model nor trend nor anything else can help in getting other orders before July. (Some such prospects in the order cycle will take longer than the minimum time, and they should also be entered into the budget as direct data.)

Similarly, if the order cycle is only three months, direct data are being misused if they are the basis for revenue for next year's fourth quarter. Unless you are quite confident of both an order and its timing from a particular customer, direct data in this case are not valid.

To illustrate the actual harmful effects of data stretching, consider a sales manager's budget that includes an order for $2,000,000 from the ABC Company next October, one year from budget preparation time. That "direct data" budget entry identifies three important "facts": customer name, order amount, and order timing. It is unlikely that things will happen just that way, but the specificity implies confidence. The organization will focus on the ABC Company order long after the prospect has disappeared, replaced, one hopes, by other prospects. The sales manager will be called upon frequently to explain the status of the ABC order and what has gone wrong. The manager's credibility will suffer. It would be much better if the sales manager had said, from trends and models, "I believe we can achieve $X of orders in the fourth quarter next year, of Y types of products, from the Z list of potential customers, but I have no way of being more specific." This is the truth, and it puts the whole organization on the same page, misleading no one. It points the sales force at a target market for target products and tells the factory the most likely range of work for which to plan.

Special Considerations

While we cannot begin to cover the specifics of every budgeting situation, a few of the more common special factors and techniques are worth noting.

Situations characterized by long-term contracts are the easiest for which to forecast revenue. If a business consists of two-year contracts, or even six-month contracts that have had a historical renewal rate of 95 percent, next year's revenue is mostly known. For new or disappearing revenue (customers who do not renew), the long-term contracts business takes on the character of either the hockey or basketball business, depending upon the nature of the business. Maintenance contracts for all the computing equipment at large government installations are an example of the former, while lawn care is an example of the latter.

Seasonal variations must be reflected in revenue forecasting, in both trend analysis and models. Businesses that budget on a calendar-year basis and have big Christmas peaks are probably the biggest budgeting challenge of all. Management does not know until year-end whether total-year results will be good or bad. If you are in such a situation, seek maximum flexibility (i.e., ability to change your budget as the relevant situation becomes better known), plan the work so that critical decisions can be made as late as possible, and possibly base the budget on a range of revenue, rather than a specific number.

Budgeting revenue in ranges rather than single values, although an appealing concept for uncertainty, generally does not work well, however. The problem is that so many numbers depend upon the revenue numbers. If you forecast ranges of revenue for each of ten products, for example, costs have to be estimated for the extremes of the ranges of all ten. In any except the simplest situations, this will yield an unmanageable range of costs and activities, equivalent to no budget at all.

Be sure to identify derivative sales relationships wherever they occur. Sales of razor blades flowing from the sales of razors are the prototype of such a situation. Captive maintenance service for products sold and software for certain computers are other examples. Plumbing distributors have found a delayed correlation of their sales with housing starts. If such a relationship can be identified, the main predictor of the sales of the derivatives is the past and forecast sales of the driving product.

Averaging revenue across a portion of the year is good budgeting practice in many situations, but understand what you have done and communicate it fully. If month-to-month revenue is quite variable and you are truly averaging, make sure that no one gets either ecstatic or depressed by good or bad results in one month.

If you are in a hockey business, try to budget orders and revenue by quarters, rather than months. Each order is too important, and its uncertainty too great, for a prediction for a given month to have much chance of being correct. If you must budget by months, always budget these large orders in the last month of the quarter. Since their timing is inherently uncertain, and top management is much more concerned about quarters than months, do not volunteer to be behind budget most of the quarter.

Be conservative when forecasting orders and revenue. A stated intent by a customer does not equal an impending order unless money has been authorized and needed approvals obtained. Remember that salespeople are optimists (or else they would not be good salespeople). Generally, they tend to be overoptimistic on the timing of a large order, even if correct about the fact of the order.

Top management always expects a correlation of the revenue budget with effort and priority. If development funds for a product improvement have been approved in the expectation of increased revenue, you had better have increased revenue for that product in next year's budget.

Finally, always factor in competitors' reactions to your new actions. If you lower prices, for example, do not forecast increased revenue based on a static situation. Competitors will react, and their expected reaction must be included in your model.

Tips and Traps

- The first thing that new managers must understand about their budget numbers is that they are the only ones who can generate them. A book can tell sales managers the best techniques for forecasting orders. Their superiors can add situational experience and amplify the general principles. But only the pertinent sales manager has the detailed knowledge to insert the numbers. New managers tend to think that there is some magic way to generate good numbers, but the only magic is in the principles and techniques, and the manager's knowledge and intelligence. No one can tell a sales manager how many orders will be obtained next year, an engineering manager how much a new design will cost, etc.—a frightening thought, perhaps, for a new manager, but nonetheless true.

- For the basketball business, frequent analysis of revenue results versus budget through the year is a particular need. The information must be there to react quickly to disappointing results with more advertising, price decreases, special sales promotions, increased training for improved service, etc. Conversely, analysis through the year for the hockey business tends to concentrate on the status of particular orders prospects.

11
Cost Estimating

Figure 11-1. Generating the numbers.

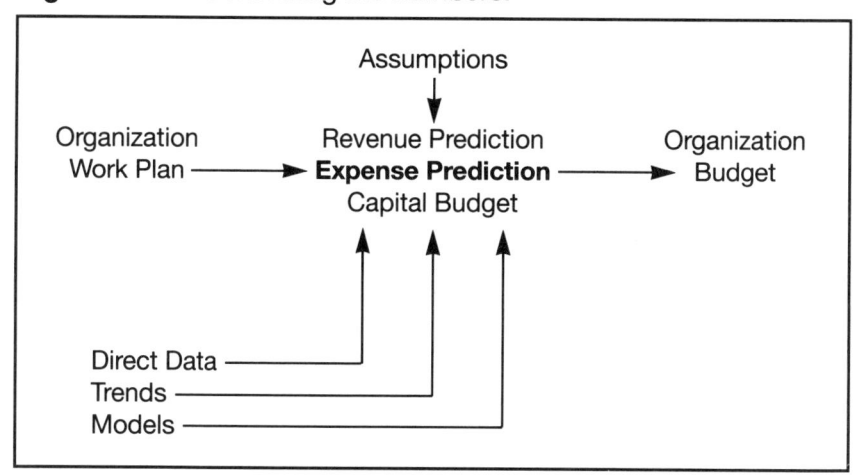

```
                         Assumptions
                              │
                              ▼
  Organization          Revenue Prediction        Organization
  Work Plan ─────────▶  Expense Prediction ─────▶ Budget
                         Capital Budget
                         ▲     ▲     ▲
                         │     │     │
  Direct Data ───────────┘     │     │
  Trends ──────────────────────┘     │
  Models ────────────────────────────┘
```

Budgeting costs is easier than predicting orders and revenue, but future costs are never totally known and controllable. There is both science and art involved in developing good cost numbers. The science is in the use of the proper principles and techniques to generate cost estimates. The art is in the specifics. There are no general algorithms that tell a manufacturing manager how much it will cost to assemble a product; the manager must understand his or her work. The combination of the principles and techniques with the manager's knowledge and experience regarding the specifics maximizes the value of the cost estimates entered into the budget.

Some managers have to budget only man-days of effort and units of purchase, and the budget analyst transforms these into dollars. However, even those managers should understand cost estimating, because dollars are the parameters on which higher managements concentrate.

Expense (cost) prediction will be considered in this chapter and is boldfaced in Figure 11-1.

The Underlying Principles

There are five basic principles for effective cost budgeting:

1. *Planning.* Budget costs are aggregates of many activity and element costs. The first step is again planning—deciding the work to be done and the unit purchases that must be made. Individual item costs must then be predicted, properly summed, and spread over time, to get budget costs.

Thus, cost estimates should be based on the planning work of budgeting, the subject of Part II. The relationships among outputs, inputs, activities, output dictators, and cost drivers are fundamental to generating the numbers for expected costs. Simply, the manager must understand the organization's work and what drives its costs if the cost predictions for next year are to be the best they can be.

2. *Proper use of direct data, trends, and models.* A number of costs are always directly predictable from data. Rent is a trivial example. Costs of most things which have been done before are in this category: mature product assembly, restaurant personnel costs, tax return preparation, etc. Things that change slowly, such as office supplies and payroll costs, should be closely predictable from direct data. Things that are bought in predictable amounts at established prices become direct data as soon as the price is known: utilities, taxes, audit fees, etc. Where valid direct data are in hand, they should always be used.

Trends are valuable for predicting the costs of things under management's control, but trends in the pertinent outside environment must be analyzed and questioned. Learning curves of all kinds are examples of the former. The cost of fuel for an airline is an example of the latter; oil prices change quickly, and recent data can be useless as a predictor. Such fuel cost is a candidate for an assumption.

Models come into play mostly in predicting costs for new activities, or new ways to do old activities. When automation is to be substituted for labor, a cost model for the automated approach is the usual and proper way to justify the capital expenditure involved. A supermarket chain will model projected costs of a new store based on knowledge and data of existing supermarkets and on local conditions for things such as rent and utilities.

3. *A large role for financial analysis people.* Operating people are inclined to miss some elements of cost. They might not include the full extent of benefits costs. Managers estimating costs of a large project might forget the costs of publishing and distributing large reports. Or they might not have the experience to evaluate the cost estimate from the publishing function, where miscommunication might result in an unreasonable estimate finding its way into the budget. The examples vary with the situation, but the problem is common.

By training and experience, the budget analyst from accounting is expert in recognizing all elements of cost in any endeavor. Managers should work closely with their budget analysts, depending on them for completeness and also a check that all the numbers appear reasonable. Indeed, managers should have a general rule that they will not submit any cost estimates until they are reviewed by the budget analyst, particularly for any new activity.

4. *Emphasis on the input side.* Where applicable (mainly manufacturing and project companies), managers should estimate and control costs on the input side (payroll costs, material costs, etc.) rather than the accountant's output side (expense, inventory, variances, etc.). Input and output accounting are discussed in Appendix A. Input accounting describes how costs are incurred in a given period, while output accounting transforms these input costs into the terms needed for the company's financial statements.

Leave the output side of the budget to the accountants. Managers should deal with costs incurred, because output parameters do not lead directly to cause and effect. For example, in a manufacturing business, some labor goes into or comes out of inventory each month. Knowing the labor that appears on the profit and loss statement as expense does not tell the manager much about the cost of labor that month. More or less may have been spent than is shown, depending upon whether inventory went up or down. The manager needs labor input to know how much was spent.

In forecasting next year's costs, managers must deal with the input world in which they manage. Estimate the costs that will be incurred—labor, material, etc. If your company requires the output form for the budget, enlist the budget analysts to make the transformation.

5. *Use of the best information available for cost estimates.* This varies with the nature of the costs, and various sources of cost information for different kinds of costs are covered in the following sections.

Purchase Costs

For things that are bought, the simplest costs to estimate are those bought at known price and quantity. An example is a magazine subscription. Simple, reliable data are available as the basis for next year's cost estimate. Known forthcoming price changes are also simple and reliable data.

When you depart from the known, expected or possible price changes require judgment, which should be assisted by the best information that can be obtained about future prices. If there is a good relationship with known vendors, they are the best source of information about their future prices. Otherwise, trends should be used, but only after analysis for changes in their causative factors. Electricity rates may have gone up, or down, for years, but that trend can change suddenly if the industry, market, or financial environment has changed for the electric utility. All available information should be used in estimating such a cost for the next year; if the information is important, uncertain, and uncontrollable, an assumption should be made.

Next in simplicity to predict are things for which firm quotations are in hand. Firm quotations from suppliers are the only fully accurate way to cost the things bought for new products or activities. Firm quotations are direct data and should be used as such.

Sometimes firm quotations cannot be obtained, and the best information available is a vendor estimate, sometimes called a "budgetary quotation." In most situations, this estimate is the best data available, and the manager's cost estimate should be based on them. However, again, judgment must be applied, because that estimate does not represent a binding commitment on the part of the vendor. As usual, all sources of information should be used: vendor past reliability, analyzed trends, industry intelligence, etc.

Then there are known things whose quantity and price will vary, such as food for a restaurant. The restaurant knows the food well, but prices vary frequently and the amount needed will depend on sales. These must be estimated, based on plans, knowledge, and experience. Data, trends, models, and assumptions must be used as appropriate. The manager responsible for buying food must use budgeted sales plus a set of outside factors (those that influence food prices locally) and restaurant actions (quality of food, buying quantities, substitution of ingredients, etc.) to predict food costs for next year. (The restaurant's annual budget, of course, can live with fairly broad estimates. The detailed, precise planning for a restaurant will probably be done on a weekly basis.)

Personnel Costs

There are two aspects of personnel costs to discuss: (1) the work to be done, and (2) the costs of the employees. A few managers are fortunate—their personnel cost budgeting consists of merely adding up the salaries of the people in their organizations. However, most have to plan the work to be done next year and then must reconcile the number and types of people in the organization with that work. The result is often requirements either for hiring new people or for laying off current employees.

Logically, the first step is to predict the work to be done in terms of the number of people required, or the man-hours (or man-days) of effort required. Then the number of people or the man-hours of effort times predicted salaries (or direct labor rates) and benefits equals the personnel cost.

Part of the prediction of the work to be done is easy, part is difficult. The effort required to do repetitive tasks that have been done before, in the same way, is easy to predict. There is known, direct data available.

Doing old tasks in a new way is the first degree of difficulty. This should be the most common personnel cost estimating problem, because managers are supposed to improve cost and performance of their organizations continuously (as discussed in Chapter 8). The new effort required follows directly from the planned activities.

More difficult is the estimation of the effort required to do new tasks or new projects. Again, the planning and definition of the work to be done (the activities) are the bases for estimating the man-hours effort or the number of people required. If the new task involves new, unfamiliar activities, they must be estimated from knowledge of similar work. If no one has such knowledge and experience, the new activities must be divided into elements to which knowledge and experience can be applied.

Consider a bank installing its first automatic teller machines. With no direct data, how does it budget the personnel costs for servicing and maintaining the machines? Possibly a consultant, or a new employee with experience elsewhere, can supply direct knowledge and experience. Otherwise, the planning must break down the service and maintenance into familiar activities, such as counting and stocking currency, preventive maintenance on electronic and electromechanical devices, and monitoring computer transactions.

The most difficult effort estimation problem is a new activity not yet definitized enough for plans to be available. This will be discussed later in this chapter.

As for the costs of employees, these are made up of wages, salaries, and benefits. Benefits are easy, often computed by the budget analyst, or calculated by the manager from a formula developed by accounting. Determination of benefits costs is accounting's problem.

Wages and salaries are budgeted in different ways in different companies, ranging from using actual salaries of specified people to using average salary rates, direct labor rates, and the like. In any case, managers must predict the wages and salaries of their people, either for specific use of calculation of the appropriate average.

A large part of the wage and salary prediction is known, direct data: the current wages and salaries of current people. Beyond this, the manager must estimate the wages and salaries of planned new hires and must subtract those due to personnel reductions.

Salary Planning

All managers must plan next year's wages and salaries in conjunction with their budgeting. (Wage planning is simply the determination of hourly rates to be paid every employee of a given classification next year. This is ordinarily done by human resources, based on the local competitive situation for different skills. Salary planning, on the other hand, is done for each individual, and is usually the manager's responsibility.) Some companies have elaborate processes for salary planning, and some have almost none. Some companies require managers to specify raises planned for each person, while others apply only an average salary increase to current salaries. In any case, a budget cannot be done without predicting next year's salaries for the organization's employees.

Compensation of salaried employees is a major management subject. It is difficult and controversial, and salary planning is possibly the least satisfying responsibility of managers. It is full of contradictions. Managements often take pride in paying well above average, while a hard-hearted owner would ask why the company should pay one dollar more than the salary that would keep an employee from leaving. Salaried Americans who work for corporations generally expect an annual raise, but do they think they deserve a raise one year before they retire?

The whole American concept of annual raises contradicts the need to constantly reduce costs. The positive motivation of merit raises has never been proved, although the negative motivation of no raises is often evident. And, theory and such contradictions notwithstanding, each of us wants and likes a raise whenever we can get one. The documented cases of Americans refusing raises are few indeed.

Fortunately, most managers do not have to deal with the theory and the contradictions in their salary planning and budgeting. Most companies promulgate guidelines, processes, and procedures for it. The manager should learn these and follow them. (There are few more important subjects in management, however. All managers should study compensation theory and practices as part of their general professional knowledge. See the Bibliography.)

Full treatment of salaried compensation is far beyond the scope of this book. However, for those unfortunates who get no guidance from their companies on salary planning, here are some basic principles:

- To budget personnel costs correctly, you must prepare a budget for salary increases. The first step is to determine what the average raise will be.

- The most important parameter of the salary planning is people's expectations. Among other things, this means that the average raise should not be changed radically from year to year without full communication and explanation of the reasons. Therefore, if you receive no guidance and company financial health has not significantly changed, use the same average raise as the previous year's.

- The amounts of planned raises should be a broad distribution. Outstanding performance should be rewarded by more than twice the average raise. No raise at all should be given for unsatisfactory performance.

- Avoid putting the planning in terms of specific raises for particular people. That implies that you have already decided how different people will perform next year. Rather, forecast a broad distribution that allows you to recognize performance as it occurs.

- Salary increases must also be budgeted in time across the year. Although different companies have different practices, raises at twelve-month intervals are probably the most common. If that is the expectation, early or late raises can send a message almost as loud as the amount of the raise.

- Undoubtedly, your budget for salary increases will have to be approved by your boss, and perhaps by human resources. If you are on your own in the planning process, be sure to allow enough time for those approvals.

New Activities Not Yet Definitized

The most difficult cost estimates are those for new activities that have been decided but not yet definitized enough for any informed prediction. The costs of new products planned but not yet designed are often in this category. New work processes for which the decision has been made but the detailed planning has not been done are probably the most common example. By definition, data and trends are not available for the new activity.

The only way to estimate costs for an undefined new activity is a judgment (really, a model) that (1) relates the new activity to something familiar, and/or (2) reduces the new activity into familiar components to which data and trends can be applied.

Consider the case of a new product planned for next year but not yet designed, requiring its costs to be budgeted. There are two ways to get at the cost estimate. First, find a current product that appears to be similar to the planned product. Absent other information, costs of the current product are probably the best source of cost information you have. Second, list the kinds of purchases and activities that must go into the new product—e.g., material, machine supplies, fabrication labor, assembly labor, and test labor. Then, again from knowledge of current and past products and activities, estimate the various elements of cost of the new product, summing them to get the total cost.

As an example of a new process, consider the fast-food restaurant that plans to start serving breakfast for the first time next summer. If detailed definition of this new offering has not been done, how can the associated costs be budgeted? Estimate food and supplies based on knowledge of prices for breakfast foods and on costs for current, similar offerings. List the various operations involved—preparing, cooking, serving, etc.—and estimate their costs based on experience with current offerings. Estimate utility costs by estimating hours of operation and business volume, and use costs for current operations that are similar. And so on.

If the new activity is a new way of doing a current task, the costs of doing it the old way must not also appear in the budget. If payroll data entry is to be automated on July 1, the first numerical budgeting step is to estimate the costs associated with automatic data entry. The second necessary step is to remove the costs associated with current manual data entry on July 1. The way to do this is to identify the activities associated with manual data entry that will disappear when the automatic data entry is implemented. The costs no longer incurred after July 1 follow directly from the identified activities. What will be done with the people totally or partially involved in manual data entry must also be planned, of course, with that planning reflected in budgeted costs.

Notice that what is being done in all cases is defining and planning the work to the best of the manager's ability. Even when definitive information is largely unavailable, there is no substitute for planning the work to be done—the starting point for all the number generation of budgeting (see Figure 11-2).

The Timing of Budgeted Cost Entries

Accountants often spread costs, to give a better continuing picture of the health of the business. A large one-time cost, for example, may be spread to the profit and loss statement (P&L) so that one-twelfth of that cost appears in each month. Or a monthly average estimate may be accrued for something like legal costs, to be adjusted later in the year if actual costs differ from the estimate.

On the other hand, managers should accurately reflect timing of costs in their budgets. If you have a large one-time cost, reflect it in the budget in the month you expect it to be incurred. Also, say a particular cost is $3X per quarter but is invoiced quarterly, not monthly. Do not average that cost $X per month; budget it as $3X four times a year, in the months that the invoice is received. And so on.

The reason is that you will be monitored and measured monthly, or at least quarterly, on your budgeted costs. Let the accountants spread and average if they like, but ensure that you present your best prediction of reality so no one will get too excited if a given month is either well

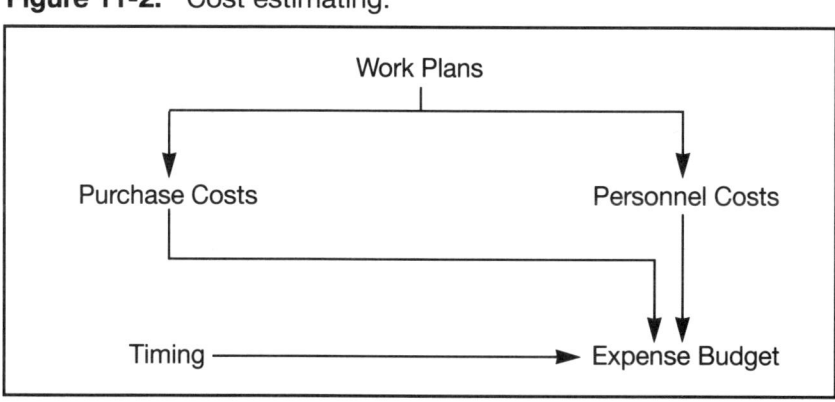

Figure 11-2. Cost estimating.

above or below budget. Also, if the accountants do spread or average your costs, make sure that you *and your boss* understand what has been done, and what your original submission was.

On the other hand, for relatively unimportant costs that vary from month to month, averaging in your budget submission may be appropriate. Just make sure that you, your boss, and accounting know that your submission is an expected average.

One of the usual rules of accrual accounting for unusual and major expenses is to charge an anticipated cost to the P&L as soon as it is known. Severance costs are accrued when the layoff decision is made, not when salary continuation is paid. Large purchases are charged when the purchase commitment is made, not when the invoice is received or paid. For the timing of budget entries for such major or unusual cost items, make sure that you put costs in the month that the accountants will enter (charge) them. Consult your budget analyst for guidance.

Accountants also add cost reserves to budgeted and actual numbers. They might reserve (anticipate) the costs of the settlement of a lawsuit, for example. A reserve more likely to affect managers' budgets is an inventory obsolescence reserve—if you are responsible for some inventory, you may be charged a monthly expense to reflect the decrease in value of that inventory with age. Such a reserve charge has to be done consistently within generally accepted accounting principles and so is the province of the accountants. Managers have nothing to do except to find out and understand what the accountants are doing to their budgets, and to again ensure that their bosses understand it.

Managers may, however, become involved with cost reserves, and sometimes should. Say that a manager recognizes the possibility, but not the certainty, of a large and unusual repair expense in next year's third quarter. Depending on the circumstances and the company's practices, the manager possibly should suggest accruing costs against that contingency during each month of next year. This is financial recognition of a possible problem, which is sometimes appropriate.

As in revenue budgeting, seasonal trends must be reflected correctly in budget cost entries. Consider the credit department of a large appliance dealer who offers extended payment terms at Christmas. A peak of collection activity will then come in February and March, requiring higher expenses for such things as overtime, telephone expense, computer time, and perhaps temporary personnel. Most organizations have some sort of variation of activity, and thus costs, across the year. No manager wants to have to explain an apparent overbudget situation that is simply the result of averaging out such seasonal variations.

The guiding principle regarding timing of budget entries is that higher management wants to understand the health and progress of the company at all times, not just the end of the year. Therefore, managers' performance versus budget will be monitored and measured monthly or quarterly. It is not enough to make good estimates of total annual costs; the estimates must also be good for each quarter and month. The accountants may blur the monthly picture with their treatments; that is not a problem as long as they and your boss understand the underlying reality of costs incurred.

Tips and Traps

- Make sure that you maintain the proper perspective in estimating uncertain costs. If an element comprises only 1 percent of your total costs, extensive analysis of it is not worthwhile. (An error of 100 percent will change your total cost by only 1 percent.) On the other hand, your major uncertain cost elements must be analyzed in depth. The penalty for a bad estimate of a major cost element is large.

- Remember that precision is not accuracy. If all you can really predict about telephone expense next year is that it will be between $50,000 and $60,000, there is no value putting $54,178 in the budget. In fact, it is harmful, because the five significant figures mislead by implying more knowledge than you have. In such a case, please put $55,000 in your budget.

- Even if your company strongly accents burden rates, never fall into the trap that says, "Direct costs are good; indirect costs are bad." A cost is a cost, and every cost decreases profit. Your goal should be to minimize *all* costs, consistent with your output requirements.

12

Capital Budgeting

Figure 12-1. Generating the numbers.

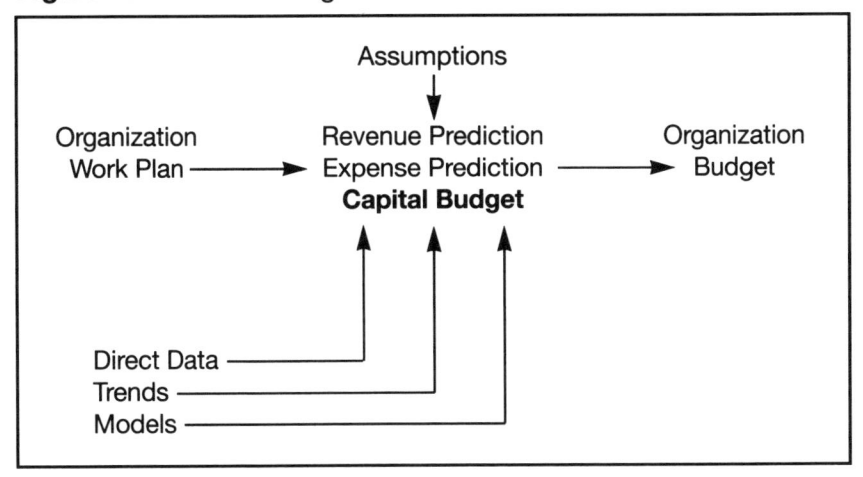

```
                        Assumptions
                             |
                             v
Organization          Revenue Prediction        Organization
Work Plan  ------->   Expense Prediction ---->  Budget
                      Capital Budget
                         ^   ^   ^
                         |   |   |
Direct Data -------------|   |   |
Trends ----------------------|   |
Models --------------------------|
```

Capital expenditures are a cost, and the discussion of cost estimating in the previous chapter applies. However, they are accounted for differently and budgeted separately from items of expense that are entered into the profit and loss statement (P&L). Capital budgets have their own processes and procedures separate from the operating budget that generates the predicted P&L. The subject of this chapter, the capital budget, is highlighted in Figure 12-1.

Factory and laboratory equipment, facility improvements, tools, and personal computers are all examples of items usually capitalized. Thus, while manufacturing, engineering, and store managers are most involved, most managers will have to do capital budgeting to some extent.

Our primary concern is to help managers cope with capital budgeting as practiced, not to find ways to compute return on investment. Our concentration is on the nature of capital expenditures and budgeting, the different types of capital expenditures and how they should be justified, and the psychological aspects of the approval of capital requests.

Capital budgets differ from operating budgets in that specific requests for capital expenditures (which will be called *capital requests*) have to be approved individually across the year. Once an operating budget is approved, managers are free to operate unless or until it is clear that the budget is being missed. Capital requests, on the other hand, usually have to be separately approved when submitted, independent of the capital budgeting process. Therefore, the nature and problems of capital requests must first be addressed, and these are the subjects of the first four sections of this chapter. The remainder of the chapter then discusses capital budgeting.

Capital vs. Expense

The concept of capital expenditures follows from the accounting principle that costs should be matched with revenue on the P&L. Consider a piece of major equipment that is expected to be used for five years in building products that will generate revenue. An erroneous picture of profitability would result from expensing the total cost of the equipment when it is purchased. That year's profit would be unrealistically low. In the succeeding four years, profit would be unrealistically high because of the use of the "free" machine. Then investors would get a shock in the sixth year, when a new machine would have to be bought and its total cost entered into the P&L.

Therefore, major expenditures for things expected to have multiyear use are capitalized and entered as assets on the balance sheet. These expenditures are then depreciated and amortized over the expected useful life, or years of use. "Depreciation" is the gradual decline in value of something because of use or age. "Amortization" is the charging of the cost of an asset (or something else) by prorating it over a specified period. (The term "depreciation" is usually used to describe the annual expense, since depreciation is the cause of that amortization.)

There are a number of acceptable methods for depreciation and amortization. A common one for public accounting is the simple straight line. If something is expected to have a five-year life, one-fifth of its cost is charged to the P&L in each of the five years. Others apply different formulas, usually designed to increase the depreciation in the early years of use.

Capital Budgeting

Fundamental to the very concept of a profit-making business is the idea of obtaining a financial return on the capital invested. The capital of a business is the equipment, tools, and the like, that result from capital expenditures, plus the other assets (cash, inventory, etc.), minus the short-term liabilities, such as accounts payable. Capital expenditures theoretically make no sense unless an adequate financial return can result from the expenditure. Thus, to be approved, capital expenditures generally must be justified in terms of return on investment (ROI).

Two words in the preceding two sentences are particularly important: "theoretically" and "generally." They are used because there are a number of categories of capital expenditures, based on the reasons for the expenditures. The problem is that the concept of ROI is not applicable to all of them, and applicable in different ways to the remainder.

Categories of Capital Expenditures

ROI is not the appropriate justification for all capital expenditures. This will be evident from consideration of different categories, starting with the simplest to justify.

Replacement of Broken Equipment

If a necessary piece of equipment is inoperable beyond repair, it must be replaced, and quickly. The ROI of this capital expenditure is not pertinent, because important activities, like production of products or services, will cease without it.

Justifying This Category

The proper justification here is the cost and performance of the recommended new equipment versus competitive equipment. In all cases of capital expenditures, cost comparisons should include predicted operation and maintenance costs over a particular period of time, which ordinarily should be the longest expected useful life of the different equipment under consideration. The residual or scrap value at the end of that time should be included. In other words, care should be taken to include *all* costs associated with the capital expenditure when making performance/cost comparisons.

Safety, Health, or Regulation Requirements

This has been an expanding category in recent years, as government regulations multiply in the areas of the environment, safety, and the like. Examples range from new factory equipment with better safety guards to a new ventilation system for the painting facility to a new entrance ramp for people in wheelchairs. As in the previous category, the return on investment is not pertinent. Such requirements must be satisfied and the only question is to find the most cost-effective satisfaction.

Justifying This Category

Also in this case, the proper justification is the cost and performance among alternative solutions of the problem. Since the required performance (satisfaction) usually cannot be compromised, this often reduces to finding the lowest cost solution. Again, total costs over a particular period of time should be used in the comparison of alternatives.

Nonquantifiable Performance Improvement

These are desirable things that will improve performance in some important way, but the improvement cannot be satisfactorily translated into a return on investment. Examples are the purchase of more powerful personal computers for all the offices, and the purchase of new equipment for the factory that will improve quality but will not reduce cost. Such items are desired either for improved performance in doing current things or for the ability to do more things. Their benefits are clear improvements in performance and professionalism, but these are difficult to express financially.

Take the example of the recent proliferation of facsimile systems in most companies. Facsimile does not reduce any recognizable cost nor ordinarily improve any recognizable profit. However, that does not make its benefits any less clear: Faster communication all around is a significant contributor to improved performance. This example illustrates that the right justification of new information technology is often the new things that can be done (some probably unknown in advance), rather than cost reduction. Computers are an obvious example of this—they seldom reduce costs, but they result in quick access to many kinds of important information not even considered for use in the precomputer days.

Justifying This Category

Justification of nonquantifiable performance improvements is difficult. There is often a temptation to try justification on the basis of cost reductions, but this quickly enters the realm of fiction and also misses the point. The only way this category will be approved is on the basis of higher management's faith that the proposing manager (1) has chosen cost-effective equipment, and (2) has the ability to achieve important performance improvements as a result of its purchase.

Cost Reduction

This is the first category in which ROI plays a valid role. Examples are buying a machine to automate tasks done manually, or buying a more elaborate machine to replace the operations of two or more current machines. (Often the motivation for purchase of new equipment is a combination of cost reduction and the next category, new capability or added capacity.) The expected cost reductions must be predicted by analysis, and the justification is that they must be sufficient to yield an adequate return for the investment in the new machine.

Justifying This Category

The mathematics of this justification take different forms in practice, although all are similar in purpose and concept. The need is to compare the ultimate, total financial result of the investment with the investment of the same amount of money for a guaranteed return.

An example of a simple technique is a *payback period* analysis. That technique determines the time it will take for the cost savings to equal the cost of the new machine. If analysis shows expected cost savings of $10,000 per month and the new machine costs $150,000, the new machine "pays for itself" in fifteen months. Top management and finance often state a maximum allowable payback period for different kinds of investments. Whether the payback is within the maximum is then the main determinant of approval or disapproval.

An example of a more complex technique is *discounted cash flow*. This technique computes the present value of a stream of future receipts and disbursements at a specified interest rate. As a simple illustration, consider the question "Would you rather have $100 today if you can invest money safely for a 5 percent return or a guaranteed $115 two years from today?" If you take the $100 today and invest it, you will have $100 × 1.05 = $105 at the end of one year, and $105 × 1.05 = $110.25 at the end of two years. It is better to choose $115 in two years, obviously. Its present value is $115/1.05/1.05 = $104.31. In other words, you would have to get $104.31 today (present value) to be *equivalent* to receipt of $115 in two years if the interest rate is 5 percent.

Business applications normally involve a number of disbursements and receipts over time (usually computed monthly), but the principle is the same. Each receipt and disbursement is "brought back to its present value" using the specified interest rate over the time period involved. Then the sum of these "element present values" is the present value of the entire stream.

The application of discounted cash flow to a cost reduction capital expenditure is that the machine purchase is a disbursement, and the monthly cost reductions are receipts. In comparing alternatives, the one that yields the highest present value is financially superior. In practice, management may set a threshold present value that all such investments must exceed to be approved.

Added Capacity or New Capability

Added capacity is needed when the company sells more than it can make. New capability means something, usually new technology, that will let the company add new product features, build higher-performance products, or otherwise serve evolving needs of customers in current lines of business. Examples abound in every industry. One example is adding surface mount technology for assembly of electronic printed circuit boards, which facilitates either smaller products or more features packed into the same size. Another example is adding equipment needed to include antilock brakes in a car model.

Added capacity and new capability are grouped in the same category because they both introduce a major uncertainty compared with the previous capital categories. Their justification ultimately depends on the revenue that can be generated from their use. Future revenue is always more uncertain than costs.

Justifying This Category

The calculations for the justification of this category are the same as for the previous cost reduction category, and payback period and discounted cash flow analyses are again good examples of techniques used. The revenue predicted over time from the new capacity or new capability is another receipt to include in the analysis.

The reasoning preparatory to the calculations, however, is much more complex. The simplest case is added capacity: Although uncertain, only the increased revenue from the same products needs to be predicted. For new capability, the reasoning branches into different situations. These can range from the "catch-up" case, in which customers are demanding the new features and competitors are already supplying them, to the "pioneer" case, in which a growing demand is anticipated for the new features. The former case is at least an easier decision, because it is almost being forced upon the company. The latter case, however, carries all the concerns of product innovation, including how much sales of existing products will be hurt. In preparing the justification calculations, expected lost revenue from current products must be included as a disbursement.

The new concept in the justification introduced by this category is that the only proper way to determine ROI is the complete life cycle of the investment. That is, all receipts and all disbursements, capital and expense, plus ultimate salvage value and disposition should be included in the ROI calculation, whether it be discounted cash flow or something else.

New Products

These are top-management decisions, but many managers are involved in the data gathering, forecasting, and analysis that supports the decision. This category is the ultimate in uncertainty. A new product can involve new customers, new competition, new activities, and so on. Such decisions are among the most difficult in business, far beyond the scope of budgeting. Here our concern is limited to the justification of the associated capital expenditure.

Justifying This Category

Justification for new products involves the same things as the previous category. Doing it over the complete life cycle is even more important; anything short of that can be misleading. The thing that separates this category from the others is the uncertainty involved in the numbers. The uncertainty is obvious for predicted revenue, but even the cost estimates are less certain than for previous categories because of the lack of knowledge and experience.

Problems With ROI Calculations

There are a number of mathematically rigorous techniques for calculating return on investment. The answers that these techniques yield are quite precise and correct, given the numbers on which the analysis is based. The problem is found in the computer adage "Garbage in, garbage out."

Any categories of capital expenditures that require ROI justification and require future revenue to be predicted for that justification are candidates for the applicability of that adage. All future revenue predictions are inherently uncertain, which can lead to elegant calculations of ROI to five decimal places, when the future revenue in the analysis had uncertainties of millions of dollars associated with it.

Precision without accuracy is the worst possible result, because there is often a faction in the company that treats ROI calculations almost as a religion. In many companies, managers are required to generate extensive and detailed numbers for ROI justification. In some companies, ROI justification and the associated effort by managers are required even for the categories to which justification does not apply.

Top managers understand the fundamental problems and limitations of such ROI analyses, of course. They still want them for the applicable categories as one input to their decision process. Some will insert their own ranges of predicted revenue, to determine, for instance, how much success will be needed to reach an acceptable threshold of ROI. But their decision will be based mostly on their judgment, whatever market and competitive intelligence is available, and their general knowledge and experience.

Generating Capital Requests

Managers' capital request problems are not the mathematical analysis and calculations involved. Managers should understand these, but the accounting people can explain them and can do them. Managers' problems are to determine the most cost-effective, needed expenditures and to develop the content and presentation of the capital request in such a way that it will be approved.

At ENLIGHTENED, INC., the different categories of capital expenditures are recognized. The capital request forms require the submitting manager to check whether the request is for replacement, cost reduction, new capacity, etc. The data and calculations required fit the different categories. At MUDDLED, INC., all capital requests must carry an ROI justification, although it is informal, with no published criteria or thresholds.

While it is easier to get a good capital request approved at ENLIGHTENED, the manager should do the same things at all companies in generating capital requests (with the exception that in some companies

Capital Budgeting 133

the manager will have to respond to inappropriate ROI justification requirements). The following steps in generating capital requests are shown in Figure 12-2:

1. Thoroughly learn your company's capital request and justification procedures. The budget analyst and your boss are ordinarily the best sources.
2. Ensure that your capital request contains the best solution to the problem you are addressing, from the point of view of your responsibilities. In some cases this will be the least cost solution, in others the highest-performance solution.
3. Include all applicable costs, operating as well as capital, over the total life expectancy of the capital item. Enlist the budget analyst to ensure that all types of costs have been considered.
4. If ROI calculation is appropriate, do such calculations in the course of preparing the request, or get the budget analyst or another person in finance to do them. You must have a good idea of the return on investment as you move through your preparation, so you can modify, improve, or abandon your request before being embarrassed.
5. If forced to do inappropriate ROI justification, first argue for an exception to policy, noting the reasons for this capital request and why ROI justification is inappropriate. If this fails, you have to stretch to find cost reductions and/or revenue enhancements that will satisfy the ROI justification requirement. The manager's

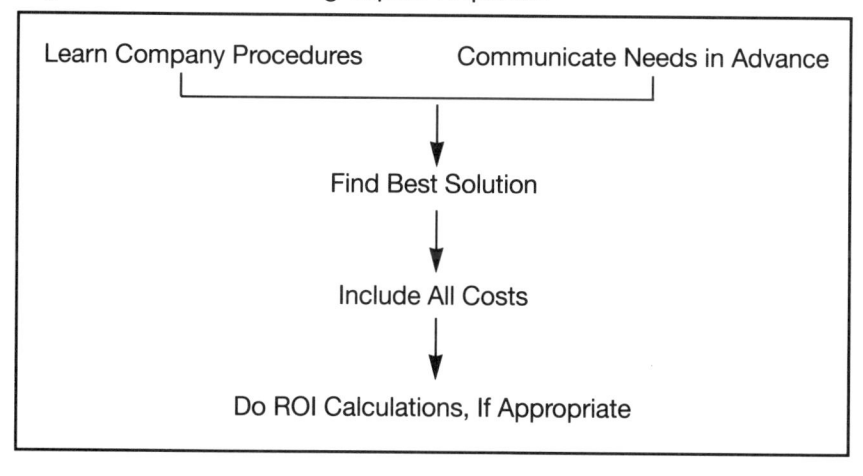

Figure 12-2. Generating capital requests.

```
Learn Company Procedures        Communicate Needs in Advance
                    |
                    ▼
             Find Best Solution
                    |
                    ▼
             Include All Costs
                    |
                    ▼
       Do ROI Calculations, If Appropriate
```

first duty is to accomplish the required work, and that involves getting the needed resources and "tools".
6. Whatever else you do or do not do, communicate your capital needs ahead of time to your boss and also to the financial people involved in analyzing the capital requests.

This last item is the key to getting your capital request approved. To get capital requests approved, your boss and higher management must understand your needs before submission, and support them.

Understand that your boss and higher management do not primarily rely on ROI calculations to decide capital expenditures. Using their experience, judgment, and knowledge of the needs of the organization, they first evaluate the cost-effectiveness of your proposal against those needs, and against their priorities and the financial constraints under which they operate. Then they factor in your credibility and the ROI calculations. The only way you can understand what they want, and what they will approve, is through continual and thorough communication about your organization's needs and the benefits of your proposed actions. This is true in general, but particularly so for capital requests.

The Capital Budget

So far we have been talking about individual capital requests, how to justify them, and how to get them approved. However, the capital budget is really the prediction of the capital requests which will be made next year. Business conditions and resulting needs change so rapidly that managers seldom know in detail what additional capital equipment they will need later in the next year.

An important point to keep in mind is that generally the capital budget cannot be exceeded, no matter what happens within broad limits during the year. The amount of the company's capital budget is a top-management decision, usually approved by the board of directors. The total amount has to be related to the balance sheet, the availability of cash, and the company's strategy. In the operating budget, there is an implicit expectation that expense will increase or decrease if revenue expands or contracts. This is generally not so for the capital budget.

Also, if the capital budget is approved by the board of directors, management has no authority to exceed it without board approval. Presidents normally try to avoid going back to the board for this. Thus, for beyond-budget capital expenditures to be approved for any manager, someone else's capital budget must be reduced. Conversely, you must be prepared to defend your capital budget through the year because you might become the "someone else" whose capital budget might be summarily reduced to provide for some other manager's capital needs.

Thus, the capital budgeting situation is that many of next year's specific capital needs are not known at budget time, but the total amount of the capital budget is almost sacrosanct. Additionally, your own approved capital budget might be reduced at any time during the year.

To make matters worse, in many companies like MUDDLED, INC., the capital budget seems almost to be a last-minute afterthought. The preponderance of attention during the budgeting process is paid to the operating budget. There may be no demonstrated connection with strategy. The total capital budget is sometimes a top-down edict, and different departments fight to get "their share" of the total. At other times it is developed bottom-up and then cut when the realities of cash and the balance sheet are perceived. Managers at MUDDLED have learned that they must submit considerably more dollars than they believe they need, because capital budgets are always cut, usually arbitrarily.

In ENLIGHTENED, INC., capital budgeting is an integral part of the entire strategy-budget process. Early in the budgeting process, a preliminary capital budget is generated, along with a preliminary operating budget. Capital needs of the selected strategy are addressed before budgeting begins, and anticipated needs of all organizations are solicited. Managers start with a good idea of the amounts and types of capital expenditures that will be favorably received. As mentioned previously, the different categories of capital expenditures are recognized and appropriately addressed. No one is surprised by submitted capital budgets; preparatory analysis and discussions have put everyone on the same page.

Generating the Capital Budget Numbers

The previous section makes capital budgeting sound like a formidable task, and often it is. Part of the problem is usually that capital budgeting does not get the attention that its importance deserves. In any company, managers involved in capital budgeting should do all of the following (see Figure 12-3):

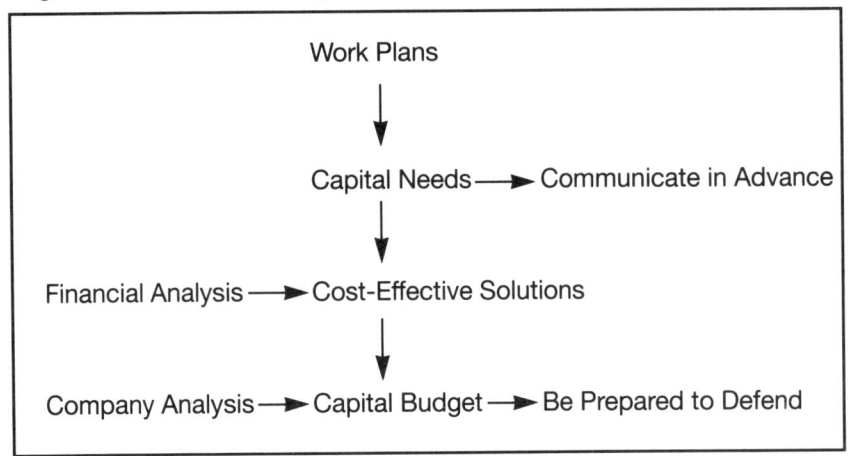

Figure 12-3. Generating the capital budget.

```
                        Work Plans
                            │
                            ▼
                    Capital Needs ──▶ Communicate in Advance
                            │
                            ▼
  Financial Analysis ──▶ Cost-Effective Solutions
                            │
                            ▼
  Company Analysis ──▶ Capital Budget ──▶ Be Prepared to Defend
```

- Learn the situation in your company: the attitude toward capital budgeting and its process, how it is established and approved, and how it is treated through the year.
- Anticipate your capital needs as an integral part of planning your organization's work, identifying next year's required outputs, inputs, and activities.
- Based on planning the work, make the best estimate you can of next year's capital needs, with as many specifics to insert as capital budget line items as possible.
- Do enough data gathering and analysis to have good numbers and cost-effectiveness comparisons for these specifically anticipated capital line items.
- Involve your budget analyst to ensure that the cost estimates are complete and to do the associated ROI calculations where applicable.
- To anticipate the level of capital budget that may be approved, analyze the trend of past capital budgets and actual expenditures, plus changes in the company's financial health and business situation. If the latter have not changed significantly, a capital budget based on the trend can probably get appproved.
- Judge the best compromise of needs and probably-approved budget level. Constitute that total number with as many specific line items as possible. Fill out the rest of the budget number with generalities: anticipated categories of needs for which you cannot be specific. (An example of such a generality is an anticipated

Capital Budgeting

level of equipment replacement due to breakdown, whose specifics naturally are unknown at budget time. This estimate should be based on the trend of such replacement, modified by knowledge of the age and condition of the applicable equipment.)
- Depending on the situation in your company, add an appropriate "pad" to the total number so determined. Support the pad with other specifics and generalities. Include some marginal items as a buffer to the important ones so that there are some easy reductions to make if required.
- Thoroughly communicate needs and the cost-effectiveness of proposed solutions to your boss and the appropriate financial people at all stages of your process. Particularly, seek to learn your boss's state of mind and this year's constraints before the process begins.
- Be prepared to defend every item in the submission, including the generalities, both during budget reviews and throughout the year.

Tips and Traps

- One of the worst management sins is surprising the boss unpleasantly. This is particularly true in capital budgeting, because your boss is probably under capital budget pressure, too. If the budget you submit is three times what the boss expected, you are almost guaranteed an emotional, adverse reaction. Communicate, communicate, communicate, well in advance.

- Capital represents the "tools"—equipment, computers, facility improvements—that can make your job easier, and whose absence can make it more difficult. Plan and carry out a year-round campaign to keep needed capital expenditures on your boss's agenda.

Part IV
Putting It Together and Selling It

13
A Manager's Budgeting Process

Managers must obviously comply with all the requirements of their company's budgeting process. We have seen that good processes, illustrated as those of ENLIGHTENED, INC., accent "thinking it through" before "crunching the numbers." Prior to generating numbers, a good process concentrates on development and communication of strategies and plans, candidates for assumptions, and definition and planning of the work to be done. Bad processes, as illustrated by MUDDLED, INC., concentrate on generating numbers with little or no preparation and guidance. In the latter, managers are subjected to severe time pressure as numbers are submitted, reviewed, modified, and resubmitted over and over again.

Budget preparation by managers is clearly easier in ENLIGHTENED. However, in any case, managers must add their own budgeting process to the company's process to ensure that all the work of budgeting gets done properly.

Review: The Work of Budgeting

A diagram of the general flow of budgeting work, which was presented in Chapter 1, is reillustrated here as Figure 13-1. The company budget is the financial expression of the company's plans for next year. It is the sum of all the budgets of the company's component organizations, suitably transformed by accounting into higher-management and financial reporting terms.

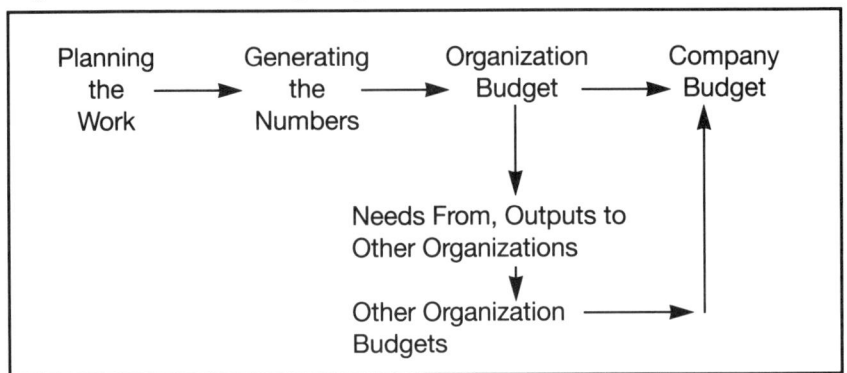

Figure 13-1. The budgeting work flow.

```
Planning  →  Generating  →  Organization  →  Company
the           the            Budget           Budget
Work          Numbers          ↓                ↑
                          Needs From, Outputs to
                          Other Organizations
                                 ↓
                          Other Organization ───→
                          Budgets
```

Organization budgets are not done, or approved, in a vacuum. They must reflect company strategies and plans, management priorities, and the needs and desires of interfacing organizations. Outputs to, and needs from, other organizations are defined in the process of planning the work and given value when generating the numbers.

"Planning the work" was expanded in Chapter 4. Figure 13-2 duplicates the earlier diagram. The goal of the planning work of budgeting is to define, for the next year, the organization's outputs (which are usually inputs to other organizations), costs, and needs (inputs) from other organizations. The timing and schedules of all these must be

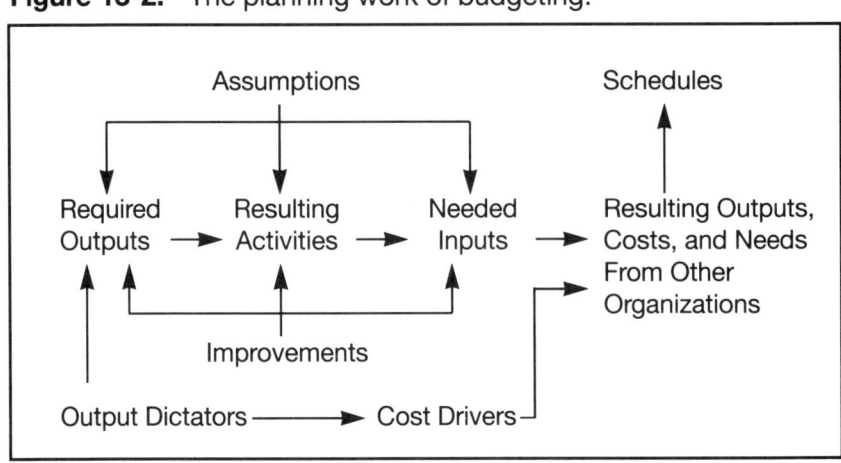

Figure 13-2. The planning work of budgeting.

```
                    Assumptions                    Schedules
                                                       ↑
           ↓           ↓           ↓                   |
Required  →  Resulting  →  Needed  →  Resulting Outputs,
Outputs      Activities    Inputs     Costs, and Needs
  ↑     ↑        ↑           ↑         From Other
  |     |        |           |         Organizations
  |     |    Improvements    |
  |                          |
Output Dictators ─────→ Cost Drivers
```

A Manager's Budgeting Process

included. The proper way to define the work is in terms of outputs, activities, and inputs, together with the things which dictate the outputs and drive the costs.

There are both deterministic and uncertain elements in this planning. The first step is deterministic: For given outputs and inputs, define the required activities and thus the costs. However, next year's outputs and inputs are never fully known at budget time. The planning must reflect that uncertainty with estimates from the best information available and explicit assumptions for those things that are uncontrollable.

The final planning step is to plan improvements (better performance, lower costs) in the way the work will be done. Improvements within organizations affect activities. Those involving several organizations—usually the improvements with the higher payoffs—can change outputs, activities, and inputs of a given organization.

"Generating the Numbers" was similarly expanded in Chapter 9. Figure 13-3 duplicates the pertinent diagam in that chapter. There are three basic kinds of numerical prediction involved in budgeting: revenue, expense, and capital. Expense and capital are both costs, but the latter involves a separate justification and approval process. (Not all managers are involved in revenue or capital budgeting, but all must budget expense.) The numbers flow directly from the organization work plan—i.e., the outputs, costs, needs from other organizations, and schedules. The sources of budget numbers in all three prediction areas are direct data, trends, and models. Explicit assumptions should supply

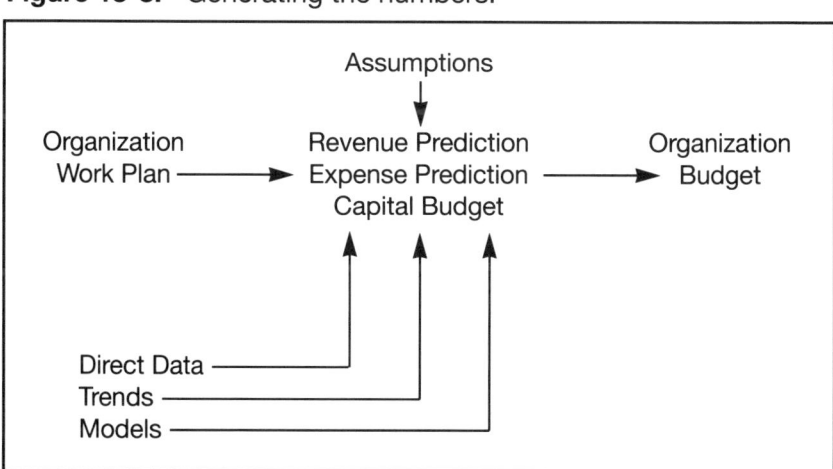

Figure 13-3. Generating the numbers.

the numbers for uncontrollable items for which none of the sources is available.

These three diagrams summarize the work managers must do to complete their budgets. The key to getting the work done is to recognize the severe time pressure inherent in most company budgeting processes. Once budgeting begins, managers can be overwhelmed by urgent information gathering and number generation. Planning the work and learning company practices must be completed before that happens. The manager's process therefore should be organized into work done before company budgeting begins and work done during the company budgeting process. We will discuss the manager's process in these terms, calling the former "preparatory work" and the latter "budget generation," with the "preliminary budget" being an intermediate step. See Figure 13-4.

Preparatory Work

To develop good budgets, managers should do the following before the company's budgeting process begins (unless you work for ENLIGHT-

Figure 13-4. A manager's budgeting process.

```
Preparatory Work
    Learn the company's budgeting process.
    Learn priorities, strategies, plans.
    Define the organization's work.
    Identify the important OEF and IUF.
    Define and conduct gap analyses.
    Model the organization's work.
    Program your personal computer.
Preliminary Budget

Budget Generation
    Obtain missing requirements information.
    Communicate with interfacing organizations.
    Finalize assumptions.
    Finish gap analyses.
    Generate the numbers.
    Communicate.
```

A Manager's Budgeting Process

ENED, which includes almost all of these items in the early stage of its company process):

- Learn the company's budgeting process, forms, terminology, and relevant accounting usage. If applicable, also learn the capital request and capital budgeting procedures. The best source for this learning is the budget analyst, plus possibly the boss and peers.

- Learn everything you can about your boss's priorities, company and division strategies and plans, accounting's priorities and points of emphasis, and the business environment and financial constraints in which the company expects to operate next year. These will never be found on one piece of paper but must be acquired by extensive reading and continuing discussions with bosses, accounting people, marketing people, and so on.

- Define the organization's current work and known forthcoming changes, in terms of outputs, inputs, activities, output dictators, and cost drivers.

- From this definition of work, identify the important outside environmental factors (OEF) and internal uncontrollable factors (IUF) that will be candidates for assumptions in the budget.

- Define the dimensions and conduct the gap analyses that will be reflected in the budget. Action programs must be developed early enough that resources for same can be included in the budget. (Gap analysis is meaningless unless the action programs are carried out.) Gap analyses can be done any time, but should be cut off at budget time, so that analysis is not changing the numbers at the same time you have to submit them.

- Model the organization's work on a personal computer, and develop any supplementary models that will help in planning, analyzing alternatives, and generating numbers.

- Program your personal computer. If your company uses paper budget forms, acquire your forms and program them into your personal computer for later ease of manipulation and modification.

If all this seems like considerable work, take consolation in the fact that every item will help you manage better. Except for the gap analysis, all these preparatory tasks are major efforts only the first time. Subsequently, all that needs to be done is to modify the results for changes.

The scheduling of this work depends on the situation. The important thing is to have it all completed when the company's budgeting process begins. If these tasks are being done for the first time, considerable effort will be required. Most of them can be done at any time during the year; new managers particularly should do this work as soon as they can after assuming their positions. If the tasks are being done for the first time, the minimum time to do all of them in most cases is probably two months, given that this is a part-time activity.

The Preliminary Budget

A practice that managers will find quite useful is the preparation of a preliminary budget as soon as possible after budgeting begins—i.e., as soon as any requirement information and ground rules are received. For a function whose outputs and work change greatly from year to year, its basis should be the personal-computer model of the organization's work discussed in Chapter 9. If the organization experiences little variability (e.g., a payroll function) just use this year's actuals, modified for known coming changes. Between these two extremes, perhaps for organizations like purchasing or branch bank operations, a combination of this year's actuals plus a few model-type relationships (equations) can be used.

As an example of the latter, a purchasing manager may conclude, in defining the organization's work, that there is a steady level of activity plus a variable component that depends on the number of new products manufactured during a year. The relationship may be something like

Incremental Man-Hours = Constant × Number of New Products,

from which incremental personnel costs—new hires and/or overtime—can be estimated. This manager's preliminary budget would then be current year actuals plus or minus amounts of different costs related to the difference between the number of new products in the current year versus the budget year.

This preliminary budget is beneficial because:

- It quickly highlights budgeting problems, such as mismatches of resources and requirements, and allows managers to focus on the most important items as budgeting proceeds.
- Together with the preparatory work, it tells managers what information they need to complete their budgets. They can then immediately concentrate on obtaining the missing information,

rather than having to spend time in defining and understanding what is missing.
- It illuminates important areas for next year, those in which performance improvements and cost reductions will have large payoffs.
- It lets managers immediately begin informed communications with bosses and peers to resolve budgeting problems and "sell" their approach to the budget and problem solutions.

If budget forms have been programmed into your personal computer, the actual generation of the preliminary budget, including analysis of a few alternatives, is easy.

Some managers are uncomfortable making the approximations and broad estimates that such a preliminary budget requires. They want to know "everything" before putting pencil to paper. However, they must understand (1) that they cannot know everything during budget time, (2) that they are smart enough to make broad estimates correctly within 10–15 percent, and that that is good enough for the purpose, and (3) that the above benefits of such a quick estimate outweight the discomfort.

Budget Generation

With the preparatory work and the preliminary budget in hand, the actual generation of the budget by inserting numbers and other requested information is straightforward. If the early work has been done well, it will not be the onerous, time-consuming task that it usually is.

The concentration during budget preparation should be on:

- Obtaining missing information regarding required outputs and inputs
- Communicating with interfacing organizations concerning needs and desires back and forth
- Finalizing budget assumptions, when needed information on required outputs and inputs becomes available
- Finishing the definition of gap analysis action programs within your own organization and with other organizations
- Generating revenue, cost, and capital budget numbers
- Communicating with the boss and the accountants every step of the way

The communication steps—with bosses, accounting, and interfacing organizations—are extremely important. That the budget cannot be done in a vacuum bears repeating. For the company to succeed, all organization budgets must be consistent and complementary. The budget is worthless if top-management strategy calls for equal emphasis on widgets and gadgets while sales budgets orders for 10,000 widgets and only 100 gadgets and manufacturing plans to build 2,000 widgets and 8,000 gadgets. Most inconsistencies are not that obvious, but they do not have to be to have bad effects on company success.

Part III discussed the various aspects of using direct data, models, and trends in generating budget numbers, and previous sections of this chapter have discussed preparatory work and the preliminary budget. The best way to put that all together in generating numbers for revenue, expense, and capital budgets is to follow these three steps:

1. Before budgeting begins, model the operation of your organization.
2. As budgeting begins use that model, and/or data on current operations, to prepare a preliminary budget based on early information about next year's required outputs and available inputs.
3. Then, as work is done and information is developed, insert direct data and questioned trends, along with the necessary assumptions, into the budget where valid and appropriate.

This process uses direct data where possible, trends where valid, and models for the rest of the predictions. It uses all pertinent information about the company, the organization, and next year as soon as it becomes available. The result will be a budget with the best possible prediction of next year's numbers, given the inherent uncertainty and uncontrollability of the future.

Tips and Traps

- The law of diminishing returns applies to budgeting. Budgeting involves a lot of work, and the tendency is to increase the work in search of better budgets. More work will not make the future less uncertain. The way to get better budgets is by doing the work recommended in this book, not by doing more work on particular elements. Experience and knowledge will make this point of diminishing returns evident to competent managers. They should cut off the work before the wheel-spinning stage; managers have other important things to do.

- Because of all the level-by-level reviews and changes, managers should keep careful notes of the assumptions, reasoning, and calculations behind each budget submission and modification. Otherwise, weeks later they may not remember the basis of a particular number when it is attacked in a new review.

- Unless you are sure of your influence and reputation, and conditions are favorable, do not make a frontal attack to try to change your company's budgeting process. The best way for the average manager to promote better budgeting is by example: Prepare good budgets and show the good results of same. Then managers can influence their bosses and neighbor organizations, thus leading their departments and divisions to better budgets.

14

Getting the Budget Approved

The final task of budgeting is selling the budget (Figure 14-1); a good budget means nothing unless it is approved. While expressed as numbers of dollars, budget approval really means the acceptance and authorization of your plans for next year, including:

- Expected and committed results
- Resources required to achieve the results
- Needed capital investments
- Action programs to generate outputs, improve performance, and reduce costs
- Support (inputs) required from other organizations

In other words, *budget approval equals approval of the definition of the job to be done next year, and of the resources required to do that job.*

There is a second aspect of budget approval that managers should seek: acceptance of the budgeting approach used. If the approach recommended in this book is accepted by the bosses, managers have a better chance of selling the right budget, and selling it on objective rather than emotional grounds. More important, if this approach is accepted, the hope is that it will be propagated to other organizations within the company. The result will ultimately be better budgeting and, most of all, better management throughout the company.

Acceptance and approval of the approach includes:

- The use of explicit assumptions for uncertainty and uncontrollability

Figure 14-1. Selling your budget.

Good Work Plans and Budget Content
Good Reputation
Good Presentations
Attention to the Company Environment
Skilled Playing of Psychological Games
Close Communication With the Boss

- The use of gap analysis for continuing improvement of organizational performance
- The use of models for number generation where appropriate, rather than direct data and trends
- The recognition of the value and validity of the definition of the organization's work, including output dictators and cost drivers.

Getting the right budget approved is not a trivial task. It requires the same level of energy and focus that must be applied to the rest of the work of budgeting. For the task of getting budget approval, we can identify three aspects: *objective, environmental,* and *psychological.* "Objective" means the independent reality and logic of the submitted budget relative to the job to be done. "Environmental" refers to situational factors outside the budget itself, such as company financial health, that affect the approval of a given budget. "Psychological" refers to the subjective factors involved, the fact that budgeting is essentially a psychological process (see Chapter 3, on the inherent problems of budgeting).

While distinct, these three aspects of obtaining budget approval are closely related and overlap in some cases. The dictates of all three must be observed; they are roughly equal in importance. However, the psychological aspect is less frequently treated, and is perhaps less obvious, than the other two.

Objective Aspects of Selling the Budget

Not surprisingly, the first requirements of the objective aspects of getting budget approval are to have justifications for all numbers and forceful arguments for all proposed courses of action. The first step in

Getting the Budget Approved

satisfying this requirement is to give the budget a logical basis by planning the work as explained in Part II, and by generating the numbers as covered in Part III.

In such a firm grounding, assumptions are particularly important and useful in the approval process. Managers should always be willing to change assumption values if their bosses so wish; the key point is to get the boss's agreement that an item in question *is* an appropriate assumption—i.e., uncontrollable by the manager and therefore something on which the manager should not be measured.

Additionally, there are personal characteristics that facilitate the objective aspects of budget approval. Approval is easier to obtain by the manager who has earned a reputation for intelligence, judgment, and integrity. Probably most important is the manager's credibility. It is difficult to overemphasize the importance of a manager's building a reputation for doing what he or she has promised. Many business plans and proposals are difficult to evaluate objectively; the planner/proposer often knows more about the subject than the reviewers. This is generally true of budgets—if you say you need ten people to do something new, the boss seldom has firm data and knowledge to dispute your estimates. Your past record in being right and accomplishing things as promised can thus carry heavier weight than anything else in the boss's evaluation.

Another important personal characteristic is having a good presentation at all budget reviews. It should be accurate, clear, well supported, and to the point. Always keep in mind that the purpose of budget presentations is to *sell*. Neither assume that it will be accepted without supporting arguments, nor drown the listener in extraneous data.

Numerical and typographical errors on presentation aids are interesting examples of credibility at work. Most bosses will accept one or two such errors without effect. Have a few more such errors and the boss will conclude you are sloppy. However, too many (and each boss has his or her own threshold) will make the boss conclude that you do not know what you are talking about. Are not such easily corrected errors a silly way to lose credibility with the boss?

The final important personal characteristic is having ready and lucid answers to the questions that arise. Here there is no substitute for knowledge of your job and of how the boss and other reviewers react to things. What are their "hot buttons," current problems, and priorities? Every budget submission and presentation should be reviewed beforehand for anticipated questions, and submitting managers should make sure that they have good answers ready for these.

Environmental Aspects

Assume that top management decides to "run out" a certain line of business, investing no more money in it but working to obtain all cash possible before it ends. Now assume that the crusading sales manager for that business line submits a budget that doubles the sales effort for next year in the belief that this business can be saved and made to grow again. That sales manager will undoubtedly have his head handed to him at the first budget review. He ignored an important environmental factor when he developed his budget: Top management has decided not to invest for growth. (If the sales manager has strong convictions about the potential for renewed growth, he has to sell that potential *before* budget time to get the "run-out" strategic decision changed.)

This is an example of the environmental aspects of budget approval at work. Managers must be aware of, and take into account, all the pertinent factors outside the objective reality of their own functions. Pertinent environmental factors include at least:

- The financial condition of the company or division
- The general state of the relevant outside environments: economy, market, competition, financial, and government regulation
- The current reputation and job security of the boss, and his or her bosses
- Company and division strategy and plans, particularly those regarding growth or deemphasis of activities in which the given organization is involved

Independent of the needs or prospects of a given organization, generally growth initiatives will not be approved if the company's financial condition is poor or the relevant economy is poor. In such cases, higher management wants cost reductions, and initiatives to increase productivity.

If your organization is part of a department that is on shaky ground, the situation is tricky. If the shakiness is due to loss of credibility of the department head, probably no aggressive initiatives within that department's budgets will be approved. On the other hand, if the shakiness is due to recent poor performance and the functions of the department are essential to the company, aggressive initiatives may be most welcome. Top management may be convinced that something different must be done within this department, and therefore is looking for such aggressive initiatives.

The environmental aspects of budget approval that are internal to the company are complex. It is often difficult, sometimes impossible, for lower-level managers to correctly discern the true internal environment. It is even more difficult for them to predict the effects on budget approval, because they are never privy to all the knowledge and resulting perspective of top management.

Therefore, there is an important caution pertinent to attempting to factor these internal environmental aspects into budgeting: Do not guess or assume you know the facts. Estimating company politics is a favorite sport of managers everywhere, and the estimates are usually wrong. Get your boss to communicate with you, and act on that communication plus whatever real data, rather than fairy tales, you can learn.

It has now been said that these environmental aspects of budget approval are important but that managers often cannot know all of the pertinent factors. That unsatisfactory situation is unfortunately the truth. So what should a manager do?

- As usual, communicate, communicate, communicate. Listen to what the boss says and to what higher management says, and watch closely what they do. Do not wait until budget submission to check an observation with the boss; do it early in the process so that you will be on the same page with him or her.

- Pay strict attention to the environmental factors that you know are true, such as a bad economy, cancellation of company credit lines, or aggressive behavior by the competition. Reflect those facts clearly in your budget. Any optional aggressive growth initiatives should ordinarily be proposed in good times, not bad times. Cost reductions and productivity improvements should be emphasized in bad times.

- Never let environmental factors overwhelm the objective aspects in required and critical items. If you are confident that a piece of capital equipment will have a good payoff in reduced cost or improved performance, never fail to propose it in the budget because of perceived negative environmental factors.

- Also, never do illogical budgeting because of perceived environmental factors. If you are convinced that you need more resources next year, never cut costs in the budget just because you believe that is what management wants. Think of the consequences if you are wrong.

- Finally, when certain environmental factors are only speculative and cannot be known, ignore them. Concentrate only on what is best for your organization, your boss's organization, and interfacing functions. The worst thing that can happen is that you will be sent back to redo the budget; you will not lose points for persuasively pushing what is best for your part of the company in the presence of a contrary indicator that you could not be expected to know.

Psychological Aspects

While you have just been told that sometimes you should ignore certain environmental factors, never ignore the psychological aspects of budgeting.

As stated in Chapter 3, the psychological nature of budgeting follows unavoidably from the conflict in objectives in which the boss wants the best results possible and to have the organization challenged while the submitting manager wants a budget that can be beaten. It also follows from the fact that both boss and subordinate are dealing with uncertainty: Neither knows what the future will hold or even exactly what resources they will need to do a specified job. With these contradictory objectives plus the uncertainty, both boss and submitting manager go through a mental process of estimating the other's state of mind.

Submitting managers must begin the thought process with good budget content, so that they know the allowable limits of the forthcoming negotiation with their bosses. After that, the first question is, "How will the boss react to these numbers?" Managers should think about the boss's attitude generally, reaction to past budgets, what he or she has said or done lately, and current pressures. Managers should also judge how smart the boss is, where the boss can be fooled, and where the subordinate had better not try to fool him or her. The distillation of all such thinking determines the transition from what the manager thinks is a realistic budget to the budget that actually should be submitted.

Bosses also get a turn, of course, and they have the advantage because they are in the controlling position and are reacting rather than initiating. Bosses consider whether the submitting managers are optimists or pessimists, the managers' records in meeting commitments, whether they are polished game players, their knowledge of the situation, and general intelligence. The boss usually has a preconceived idea of approximately what the subordinate's budget should be, and this is ordinarily modified somewhat by good subordinate input.

Boss and submitting manager eventually arrive at an agreed budget, with which each has varying degrees of comfort. As in any negotiation the result is probably better if both sides have roughly an equal degree of discomfort.

How should the submitting manager, armed with good plans for next year's work and good budget content, play this psychological game? It depends on the nature of the manager's boss and the relationship between manager and boss.

The best situation is the one that allows the manager to be straightforward and objective. If the boss is competent and reasonable, and the relationship is good, this is the recommended approach. The subordinate manager's cost estimates, after all, are intellectually, not emotionally, grounded. The best budget will result if the arguments are about specific outputs, activities, inputs, or assumptions. These are the arguments that bosses and subordinates are supposed to have, and they and the company will be better off if these are the arguments joined in budget negotiations.

On the other hand, if the conditions of good relationship with a good boss are not present, managers must protect themselves. They should still base their arguments on the planning and definition of their work and on associated assumptions. However, it is difficult to overcome emotion with logic. If managers believe that their budgets will be subjected to emotional attack (and if they do not know, this is the safest assumption to make), they should "pad" their budgets discreetly and cleverly as a defense against emotion and arbitrary cuts.

Such padding is the enemy of good budgeting, but the manager's first responsibility in budgeting is to get approval of the resources needed to do next year's required work. It is seldom as simple as adding 5 percent to everything because the boss is known to make 5 percent arbitrary cuts. It usually takes all the intelligence and perception that the subordinate manager can bring to bear.

Selling Your Budget

In short, the best basis for getting your budget approved is concentrated attention on the following:

- Proper intellectual grounding of the budget in the organization work plan and the use of the best sources for budget numbers
- A good reputation and good presentations
- Appropriate attention to environmental factors
- Skilled playing of the psychological games
- Close and continual communication with the boss

The obvious, gross basis for the last requirement is that one of the worst things you can do is surprise the boss unpleasantly at budget time. That is almost guaranteed to make the budget negotiation emotional. However, a basis that is just as important is that the boss will understand the manager's budget because the boss was privy to the manager's reasoning as it developed. And the manager will understand the boss's state of mind, and the degree of approval or disapproval of various items, before budget reviews begin.

Alas, the most perfect implementation of these directives cannot guarantee budget approval. The psychological world of budgeting can be full of surprises, and the pertinent environmental factors (also partly psychological) can never be fully known. Still, the recommended process for selling your budget will give you the best possible chance for approval, and also put you in the best possible position to react to any surprises that the budget approval process brings.

Tips and Traps

- The credibility that results from consistently delivering what has been promised is an extremely important attribute for a manager, one to be nourished and guarded most carefully. Sadly, many managers do not realize its importance until too late—that is, until they have ruined their credibility by *not* delivering as forecast too many times. They should then not wonder why they have more trouble than their colleagues in getting the boss to approve their proposals.

- Final tip: Take budgeting seriously. Better budgeting can increase your job satisfaction, make you better able to cope with the problems that will undoubtedly arise next year, and enhance your management career.

Appendix A
The Language of Accounting

While budgeting is a management activity rather than an accounting activity, the results are expressed in accounting terms. Therefore, to understand budgeting, the manager must understand the aspects of accounting that are used in budgeting.

This appendix is selective, in no way constituting a summary of the fundamentals of accounting. To do a budget, managers must understand why revenue and expense are different from cash flow, and what a burden rate is and how it is used. However, they do not need to know any of the accounting rules that apply to preparing balance sheets. Readers wanting the latter information should consult a book on accounting fundamentals—see the Bibliography.

One purpose of accounting is to correctly and usefully portray the financial health and success of a company. In this sense, the final products of accounting are the *financial statements*. The need for financial statements is more obvious for a public company. Its many, remote owners (stockholders) need standardized information to maintain knowledge of the health and success of the company in which they have invested. However, private companies have the same need if they have to borrow money or want to compare themselves with other businesses. The main financial statements of concern are the cash flow statement, the balance sheet, and the profit and loss statement. Figure A-1 outlines the topics discussed in this Appendix.

Figure A-1. The accounting language of budgeting.

Cash Flow
The Balance Sheet
Profit and Loss Statement (P&L)
    Revenue
    Expense
Allocated Costs, Cost Burdens, and Burden Rates
Valuation of Inventory
Input and Output Accounting
Standard Costs and Variances
Return on Investment (ROI)
Margins

Cash Flow

As a small business begins, its owner's main financial concern is cash—how much the company has, how much it needs, how much it will get in a given period of time. *Cash flow* for a period of time is the amount of increase or decrease in a company's cash during that period. (In business usage, "cash" means checks and other monetary instruments, as well as currency.)

$$\text{Cash Flow} = \text{Receipts} - \text{Disbursements}$$

Receipts are cash taken in, while disbursements are cash paid out.

Cash flow is the simplest concept in accounting. Receipts and disbursements are never called anything else, and they are recorded when they happen.

Cash flow remains important for any business of any size, because cash is the ultimate survival parameter. However, it is not the best financial measure of a business. Negative cash flow is not necessarily bad. It can be good if it results from buying new products that will result in more retail store sales, or from buying new equipment that will yield increased sales by a manufacturer. Similarly, positive cash flow is not necessarily good. If it is the result of selling magazine subscriptions paid in advance, you do not know whether it is good or bad until all the contracted magazines have been delivered and you know what they cost to produce.

Most businesses, including all public companies, use *accrual accounting*. Cash accounting records revenue, expense, and changes in balance sheet accounts when cash is received or paid. Accrual accounting, in contrast, records revenue when earned and costs, generally, when a commitment to spend is made. Also, costs paid once a year can be "accrued" in equal amounts each month. Accrual accounting gives a more realistic picture of the health of a business by focusing on commitments and by "spreading" large, infrequent costs.

The Balance Sheet

If you start a business with $5,000 cash and spend $500 on a machine and $500 on materials, your cash flow is a negative $1,000. However, the value of your new business is still $5,000. You have merely exchanged $1,000 of the cash for $1,000 worth of equipment and materials that will be used to make money.

The financial statement that portrays the health of a company is the *balance sheet*. The basis of the balance sheet is the accounting equation

$$\text{Assets} = \text{Liabilities} + \text{Equity}$$

Assets are those things of value that a company owns. Liabilities are things of value that the company owes to someone. Equity is then what the company is worth. (The terms "net worth" and "shareholders' equity" are generally used interchangeably for equity, although strictly speaking the former applies to a proprietorship while the latter applies to a corporation.) Rearranging the accounting equation yields:

$$\text{Equity} = \text{Assets} - \text{Liabilities}$$

or, in plain English,

$$\text{What You Have} = \text{What You Own} - \text{What You Owe}$$

Typical assets of a company are cash, securities owned, accounts receivable (money owed to the company for products and services already delivered), inventory (the company's stock of materials and/or products that eventually will be sold), equipment, and land and buildings owned. Prepaid expenses are also assets, because until used they have value: the right to the use of something in the future. For example, if rent for some reason were paid for a year in advance, the payment would ordinarily be recorded as an asset which decreases (is "expensed") by one-twelfth every month.

Typical liabilities are accounts payable (money that the company owes for things bought and received), debts of all kinds, and advance payments for products and services. The latter are a liability because the company has an obligation to supply a product or service in the future in return for that payment. The magazine subscription payment received, for example, represents a liability, to be partially discharged every month by delivery of a magazine.

The equity of a company is its value in terms of the results of all past transactions. However, real value is whatever people are willing to pay for the company or its shares at a given time. "Market value" may be more or less than "book value" (i.e., equity), depending upon what potential investors believe the company's prospects to be.

In presentation, assets are divided into current assets (cash and those things readily convertible into cash) and fixed assets (nonmonetary, mostly tangible things). Liabilities are divided into current, or short-term (obligations that must be discharged within a year), and long-term (those that must be discharged in more than a year).

Profit and Loss

The vehicle used to describe the success of a company is the *profit and loss statement (P&L)*. This is also called the operating statement or the income statement. While the balance sheet describes a company at a given point in time, the P&L describes results of operations over a period of time: a year, a quarter, or (internally only) a month. (Cash flow also describes results over a period of time.)

The main purpose of the P&L is to provide a realistic measure of the current success of a business by properly reflecting timing of the effects of receipts and disbursements. The equation for profit is

$$\text{Profit} = \text{Revenue} - \text{Expense}$$

Loss is a negative profit.

Revenue

Revenue is the dollar value of what the company sells but will not equal receipts until after a business is ended, because of the timing differences necessary to reflect properly the degree of company financial success.

For the case of the magazine subscription, success (profitability—i.e., how much money the magazine publisher makes) would be unrealistically portrayed if the advance payment were recorded as revenue when received.

A better picture would be obtained if nothing were recorded until all the magazines had been delivered. Then the actual costs to produce and deliver all the committed magazines could be subtracted from the price of the subscription, giving a true picture of how much money the publisher made from that subscription. However, public companies have to report results quarterly and annually. If the subscription were for two years and not recorded as revenue until completed, there would be no recognition in the P&L of the piece of business represented by this subscription through one annual report and seven quarterly reports. This would also give a misleading picture of the publisher's current degree of success.

To give the most realistic picture, the normal accounting practice is to record revenue as each magazine is delivered. For a two-year subscription to a monthly magazine, one twenty-fourth of the subscription price is recorded as revenue each month. The costs to produce and deliver the magazine each month are then recorded on the P&L as expense for that month.

Rather than being paid in advance, more businesses sell on credit and are paid sometime after the customer receives the product or service. Again, however, the principle is that revenue is recorded when it has been "earned"—when the product or service has been accepted by the customer. If revenue were not recorded until receipt of payment, it would vary with collection terms and customer payment practices. This again mixes other considerations into the basic question that the revenue number answers, which is "How much did the company *sell?*"

There are almost as many ways to record revenue as there are kinds of businesses. Companies that work on large construction contracts or large military systems and those that sell expensive products with long manufacturing times often use the "percentage of completion" method. In this scheme, revenue is recorded in each month of the long project in proportion to the progress made on the job. The reasoning is that waiting until the end of a long project would make the company look less successful than it really is for a long time, followed by a big revenue spike which would look like a windfall and confuse investors.

Expense

The timing considerations that go into recording expense are even more complex than those for revenue. Producing our example magazine requires a variety of costs, with various treatments as far as recording on the P&L is concerned. The purpose, again, is to align the expense and revenue with the timing that gives the most realistic picture of current business success. For one magazine, let's consider four kinds of costs that illustrate different accounting treatments: the cost of the equipment that prints the magazine, of the paper on which it is printed, the wages and salaries of the people involved in producing the magazine, and rent.

The printing equipment was bought and paid for years ago. Is it then free as far as this magazine is concerned? No, that would make the magazine look more profitable than it really is. If the equipment were not there, it would have to be bought to print the magazine. If that were the case, would you charge the entire cost of the printing equipment to this one magazine? No, that would be equally misleading. Such equipment is an investment needed and used to produce revenue over a number of years, so it is recorded when bought as "capital" of the company.

The cost of the equipment when bought was a *capital expenditure*. A "useful life" (the period of time before it would wear out or have to be replaced by newer technology) was estimated for it at that time. The equipment would then be "depreciated" over that useful life and its cost "amortized," or spread, over that same time period. There are various acceptable ways to do this, but a common, simple way is called straight-line depreciation: If the useful life is five years, one-fifth of its cost is charged to expense in each of those five years.

Generally, anything that is used in the business more than one year is capitalized: factory equipment, tools, computers, improvements to the facility, and so forth. Capital expenditures have to be budgeted separately because of the different accounting treatment they receive.

Regarding the paper used for the magazine, it is bought periodically in large quantities and stored until used. Again, a misleading picture of pofitability would be given if the paper is "expensed" when bought. A better picture is obtained if it is expensed when it is *used*. While in storage the paper also has value; presumably, it could be sold if never used. Therefore, the paper when bought is recorded as an asset called *inventory*, which is the stock of valuable materials (or products, in the case of a retailer or distributor) that the company will eventually use to produce revenue. When paper is used to print the magazine, the amount used is recorded as expense and the inventory reduced by an equal amount.

The wages and salaries of the people directly involved in printing the magazine are called *direct expense*; the labor component of direct expense is called "direct labor." Rent is an example of costs that are independent of the production of a given magazine. These are generally called *indirect expense,* meaning costs needed to run the business but not directly involved in producing revenue.

If the publisher is selling only one magazine, there is no need to distinguish between these two types of expenses. However, if more than one type of magazine is being sold, the publisher wants to know the profitability of each. Therefore, a mechanism is needed to assign costs to the different products. The direct expense is assigned to a given magazine as incurred. However, by definition, the indirect expense cannot be so directly charged. Therefore, some formula is needed to allocate the indirect expense realistically to different products. This leads to the concept of cost burdens and burden rates, covered in the next section.

Timing also enters into the charging of direct and indirect costs to the P&L. If a magazine is printed this month and sold next month, its direct costs are put in inventory this month and charged to the P&L next month. The underlying principle is again to match revenue and expense. No matter when and how rent is paid, a constant amount each month is probably charged to the P&L to reflect the reality of a constant, monthly cost of doing business.

This simple magazine example is sufficient to illustrate the various ways in which costs are categorized. In the real world, classification into capital, inventory, direct, and indirect costs, as well as the timing treatments of them, gets complex and somewhat arcane. Also, the Generally Accepted Accounting Principles (GAAP) that govern how the accounting is done are sufficiently flexible such that different companies can apply them in different ways.

Different Expense Treatments

While the magazine example is illustrative, different types of expense treatment are appropriate for different kinds of businesses.

Almost all businesses have capital expenditures. These are particularly important to utilities, in that the regulated rates they can charge are generally determined by the capital they have invested.

Generally all businesses that sell nonperishable products have inventory. (Perishable products are used or sold too rapidly for inventory to have any meaning in the accounting sense.) Businesses that work on large labor contracts may also have inventory, to account for timing adjustments in recording P&L expense. On the other hand, inventory is generally not a meaningful concept for most service businesses and utilities.

The use of, and distinction between, direct and indirect expense has narrower usage. It is generally limited to manufacturers and companies whose business consists of project contracts of various kinds: military systems, construction, maintenance of equipment, etc. The distinction is a way to understand the profitability of a relatively small number of different products. For retailers, distributors, financial service firms, and very small companies in general, the concept is usually not appropriate.

Allocated Costs, Cost Burdens, and Burden Rates

Most companies allocate some costs in some fashion. These appear in a manager's budget after the first submission, having been apportioned and inserted by the budget analyst.

A chain of retail stores probably allocates corporate expense to each store. Many companies allocate the costs of international sales to all the divisions and products that sell internationally. The cost of the Washington office of a pharmaceutical company may be allocated across all the product divisions.

The principal motivation for allocation of costs is to give management a better picture of the profitability of different businesses and products. Many formulas for allocation are used, some simple (like allocating cost proportional to the sales of different products or stores) and some complex (like analyzing activities and allocating costs of different activities to the business outputs which cause them).

A second motivation is for accounting to be in compliance with GAAP. The accounting principles are flexible; within broad limits, any formula is all right as long as there is consistency, and changes in allocation formulas have to be justified to the auditors.

A category of costs allocated by many companies is *general and administrative expense (G&A)*. G&A is often a second "layer" of indirect expense, so to speak. The first "layer" is indirect costs that are closely associated with producing revenue but cannot be identified with individual projects and products. Examples of first-layer expense in a factory are the costs of manufacturing engineering, purchasing, planning, and salary of the factory manager. These are usually called "manufacturing overhead." Similar costs in other functions might be called "engineering overhead," "service overhead," "operations overhead," etc.

G&A, the second layer, is those costs needed to operate the business but not closely associated with producing revenue. Examples are costs associated with the president and board of directors, the finance department, and human resources. (Smaller businesses might just call all of this "overhead.") They are necessary costs that must be covered by the company's revenue, but they exist essentially independent of what or how many products are produced.

ENLIGHTENED, INC., allocates G&A costs to different businesses and products based on an analysis of their drivers (causes). Such activity-based costing is a relatively new technique that relates business outputs to all activities required to produce the outputs. Such a technique gives management the best possible picture of the profitability of each of its activities and businesses.

However, activity-based costing is not yet in general use. Most companies use a much simpler formula for G&A allocation, which introduces the concepts of *cost burdens* and *burden rates*. A cost burden is an amount of one type of cost added to another on the basis of a formula. A burden rate is simply the percentage rate at which a cost burden is assigned. For example, a common practice in military systems companies is to allocate G&A to different projects in relation to their sales. In this case the burden rate is the "G&A rate," which is

$$\text{G\&A Rate} = \text{G\&A Expense} / \text{Total Sales}$$

The cost burden on a particular project by G&A is then the G&A rate multiplied by the sales of that project. In other words, the cost of each project is "burdened" with a proportion of the total G&A expense, based upon that project's proportion of total sales.

The most complexity relative to cost burdens and burden rates is again usually found in manufacturing and project contract companies. This is where the distinction between direct and indirect costs is found, and where *overhead expense* clearly distinct from G&A is most obvious. In factories, direct labor costs are often burdened with "manufacturing labor overhead" (e.g., planning and production control costs), and direct material costs are often burdened with "manufacturing material overhead" (e.g., purchasing and material handling costs). The manufacturing labor overhead rate would be the total indirect costs in the "labor overhead pool," as defined, divided by total direct labor. Each dollar of direct labor would then be burdened with dollars resulting from multiplying the direct labor dollars by the labor overhead rate. In equation form:

$$\text{Labor Overhead Rate} = \text{Applicable Indirect Cost} / \text{Direct Labor Cost}$$

and

> Labor Expense = Direct Labor Expense + (Direct Labor Expense × Labor Overhead Rate)

Thus, if the labor overhead rate is 200 percent, every dollar of direct labor expended on a project will result in a labor expense to that project of $3. That is, $1 + ($1 × 200 percent).

In these manufacturing and project businesses, under traditional accounting, direct costs are always burdened with indirect costs. Again, ENLIGHTENED, INC., has done the work necessary to relate activities to outputs and does not even use the direct and indirect cost terminology. However, ENLIGHTENED is still the exception rather than the rule.

Special Problems of Manufacturing and Project Companies

In manufacturing companies, the realistic *valuation of inventory* is complex. Typically, a piece of material received from a vendor goes into "raw materials" or "stores" inventory. After it is worked into a subassembly on the factory floor, it can go back into inventory as "work in progress." A given piece of material might go through multiple stages of "work in progress," increasing in value at each state. When the final product is complete, if it has not yet been sold, it goes back into inventory as "finished goods."

For a realistic valuation of the inventory, the labor expended in those stages should go into inventory with the material, because that labor was expended usefully but not for a product that has been sold yet. The same is true for indirect costs: They are incurred because of that work that causes direct labor and material to go into inventory.

Manufacturing businesses—and project businesses, because they also put direct cost into inventory for recording on the P&L in a different period—thus use *input accounting* and *output accounting*.

"Input accounting" describes how costs are incurred in a given period: direct labor, direct material, indirect costs, etc. This is how costs must be controlled by the managers directly responsible for them, such as the assembly manager. "Output accounting" combines and transforms these input costs into the terms in which they go into the P&L and the balance sheet. The company is measured on the output form, and therefore that is probably how the president measures the vice-presidents.

Consider direct labor. In a normal period, work is done on products shipped (or projects completed) and recorded as revenue, and on products (projects) put back into inventory for later completion and shipment. Also, some previous costs are taken out of inventory for previously built products now delivered as revenue. Thus, a portion of the direct labor cost incurred during a given period goes into the P&L and a portion goes into inventory. Likewise, the direct labor expense on the P&L includes some cost incurred during the period and some labor expense taken out of inventory. In other words, the "output accounting" for direct labor on the P&L is normally different from the "input accounting" for direct labor cost incurred during the given accounting period. The same thing applies to direct material, in the same way.

Indirect costs are recorded as incurred in "input accounting," but show up on the P&L only as burdens to direct labor or material expense. These burdens also go into and out of inventory with the direct costs.

Some such companies further complicate the relationship between input and output accounting by using *standard costs*. A standard cost for a product is its expected cost to produce. If used, the standard cost is what goes into the P&L and into inventory for that product. If actual costs differ from standard costs, a *variance* results as an item in output accounting. Variances ordinarily have to be expensed during the month incurred. (Budgeted variances are ordinarily zero, almost by definition. They arise in cost reporting across the year.)

Thus, for these types of companies, budgets are not only consolidated but greatly transformed as they rise up the organization. The assembly manager needs budgets and financial reports in the input form. However, the vice-president of manufacturing needs both the output form (on which the president will measure him or her) and the input form (to manage and control the organization).

Financial Measures

The final aspects of accounting that the manager needs to understand for budgeting are the various ways used to express financial performance.

The most common measure of a company's financial performance is "return on (something)." ROE is "return on equity":

$$ROE = Profit / Equity$$

ROC is "return on capital":

$$ROC = Profit / (Equity + Debt)$$

ROE would be the primary concern of an individual considering starting a business rather than leaving money in a money market fund. Equity measures the value of the investment in the company, so the investor would want a higher ROE from the new company that he or she could get from the money market fund. Large, successful companies presumably can make more profit by borrowing money to invest in the business, so ROC is often considered a better measure of such a company's performance. Return on assets (ROA) is also sometimes used.

Most managers probably will not get involved with these measures in budgeting, but they may have to deal with *return on investment (ROI)*. In proposing capital expenditures, often managers have to justify them in terms of the ROI that the proposed capital investment will yield, among other things.

There are many ways in which return on investment is approached. For a company as a whole for a given period of time, ROI = ROC, by definition. For a new product development, life cycle ROI is appropriate and probably required—i.e., the ratio of all receipts to all disbursements (including the initial investment) over the total life of the product. Sometimes the break-even point is wanted—i.e., the amount of time needed to recover the investment, usually expressed in terms of cash.

The areas of financial measures that most involve managers in budgeting are *burden rates* and "margins" of various kinds. Some burden rates, like G&A, are just applied to a manager's budgeted costs, without input or recourse. The important ones from a measurement viewpoint, however, are those for which the manager has partial or total responsibility. Examples are the engineering overhead rate for an engineering manager and the material overhead rate for a purchasing manager. Many companies regularly scrutinize these burden rates and strongly measure managers on their ability to minimize them, making budgeted rates important to the managers.

Various *margins* are used as financial measures. A margin is a percentage measure of profitability relative to sales. (Sometimes "margins" are expressed in terms of dollars. We use "margin" strictly for percentages, and use "gross profit," "contribution," and "profit" to describe dollars.) Probably the most common margin used is "gross margin":

Gross Margin = (Sales − Cost of Goods Sold) / Sales

"Cost of goods sold" usually means direct costs burdened by functional overheads but not by G&A. (Again, this varies by industry—some distribution companies include only material costs in the gross margin calculation.) Gross margin of a product is thus a measure of the profitability of that product with its costs defined in a certain way.

Another common margin is "contribution margin":

$$\text{Contribution Margin} = (\text{Sales} - \text{Direct Expense}) / \text{Sales}$$

The difference, obviously, is that contribution margin ignores cost burdens and allocations.

"Profit margin" is simply

$$\text{Profit Margin} = \text{Profit} / \text{Sales}$$

Profit margin is often referenced in financial writings about companies but is mainly important relative to past performance or to the performance of competitors. ROE and ROC are generally the more important measures for investors.

Accounting and the Budgeting Problem

Most managers are not involved with the balance sheet in budgeting. It is usually the province of finance, using activity numbers supplied by managers. Relatively few managers must budget cash flow. The P&L is the arena for most of the work of budgeting for most managers.

Concerning the P&L, managers need to know how their companies apply the general concepts discussed here: the ways costs are accumulated, particular burden rates used, margins and other financial measures used, etc. These can be learned only inside the company, the best source being the budget analyst and other accounting personnel.

Managers must also understand the relationships that drive the burden rates, margins, etc., with which they must deal. For example, a manager responsible for a product should know that contribution margin varies only with the direct costs of that product. However, because it includes cost burdens, gross margin varies with the revenue and costs related to all products included in the burden rate calculation.

Many managers are involved in the capital budget, which has its own rules and techniques, treated in Chapter 12.

Appendix B

Glossary of Accounting Terms Used in Budgeting

accounts payable Amounts owed by a business for purchases received and accepted.

accounts receivable Amounts owed to a business by customers for goods and services received and accepted.

accrual accounting An accounting basis in which revenue is recorded when earned and costs and balance sheet account changes are recorded when commitments are made. Large, one-time expenses can also be averaged over the year or a portion thereof.

accrued cost A cost recorded as expense that represents future actual expenditure.

accumulated depreciation The total depreciation of a fixed asset from its purchase to the present time.

allocated cost Cost of one type that is assigned or charged to costs of other types.

amortization Charging the cost of an asset, liability, or expenditure by prorating over a specific period.

asset Anything owned that has monetary value.

backlog Orders that have been received but not yet delivered; also called sales backlog or orders backlog.

balance sheet A financial statement showing the assets, liabilities, and equity of a business as of a certain date.

book value The current accounting worth of a business or a balance sheet item. For a fixed asset, it equals cost minus accumulated depreciation. For a business, it is the same as equity, net worth, or shareholders' equity.

budget The financial expression of the plans and expected results of a business for a particular period of time, conventionally a year.

budgeted cost The expected cost of an activity during the budget period.

burden rate The percentage rate as which a cost burden is added to particular other costs. The most common burden rates are the various overhead rates.

capital The investment in a business, ordinarily equal to equity plus debt.

capital budgeting The prediction of fixed asset investments that will be needed during the budget period.

capital expenditure The amount required to purchase equipment, tools, and the like, that will be accounted for as fixed assets and depreciated over a multiyear period.

cash Currency and monetary instruments that are equivalent to currency.

cash accounting An accounting basis in which revenue, expense, and balance sheet items are recorded when cash is paid or received.

cash flow The increase or decrease in the cash of a business over a particular period of time.

chart of accounts A list of the accounts used in a business for the process of accounting.

contingent liability A possible liability.

contribution margin A percentage measure of profitability, equal to revenue minus variable or direct costs, divided by revenue. (The term is sometimes used for the dollar amount of revenue minus variable or direct costs, although the latter is more often called contribution.)

corporate cost A cost pool that includes the costs incurred by the headquarters activities of a corporation, usually allocated to divisions and product lines in some fashion.

cost The amount of money spent to do or to buy something.

cost allocation The process of assigning or charging one type of cost to other costs.

cost burden The amount of cost added to a particular cost as the result of allocating another type of cost to it.

cost center A unit of an organization for which costs are budgeted and collected, implying measurable characteristics of performance and responsibility.

cost of goods sold The direct costs of producing revenue, burdened by closely associated indirect costs. Also, beginning inventory plus purchases minus ending inventory. Often called cost of sales or cost of revenue.

Glossary of Accounting Terms Used in Budgeting

cost pool A grouping of costs for the purpose of allocation to, or identification with, particular cost centers, products, or services. Common cost pools are various overhead costs, general and administrative costs, and corporate costs.

current assets Assets that will have value, or will be converted to cash or other assets, only during a current period, typically a year.

current liabilities Debts and payments that are due within a year.

current ratio The ratio of current assets to current liabilities.

days inventory The amount of inventory relative to the cost of goods sold, expressed in "days," typically as 365 times inventory divided by annual cost of goods sold.

days payables The amount of payables relative to total material purchased, expressed in "days," typically as 365 times accounts payable divided by annual material purchases.

days receivables The amount of accounts receivable relative to revenue, expressed in "days," typically as 365 times accounts receivable divided by annual revenue.

debt Broadly, any liability. More narrowly and more commonly, money borrowed from, and owed to, another person or institution.

depreciation The gradual decline in value of an asset because of use or age; also, the expense arising therefrom.

direct cost Cost directly associated with production of specific revenue.

disbursement An amount of cash paid out.

discounted cash flow The present value of a series of future receipts and disbursements, at a specified interest rate.

equity The accounting value of a business, equal to assets minus liabilities. Commonly used interchangeably with book value, net asset value, net worth, and shareholders' equity.

expense Cost that is charged to profit and loss during a period, in accordance with generally accepted accounting principles.

financial statement An accounting document showing the financial status of a business, or the results of business activity.

finished goods inventory The portion of inventory that consists of goods and products ready for sale, and that includes their total costs.

fiscal year The twelve-month period for which financial results are prepared and reported. It may be different, by company choice, from the calendar year.

fixed assets An asset—such as machinery, land, buildings, and the like—whose life will extend beyond the current accounting period.

fixed cost A cost that does not vary with revenue over a relevant range of revenue amount.

fringe benefits   Payments by a company for things of value to, and for the use of, employees, such as insurance and vacations.

general and administrative expense, or cost (G&A)   Cost necessary to operate a business but not associated directly with the production of revenue or with particular functions of the business. Typical G&A costs are those associated with the president and board of directors, the finance department, and human resources.

Generally Accepted Accounting Principles (GAAP)   The set of rules by and for the accounting profession that govern accounting practice and the preparation of financial statements.

goodwill   A depreciating asset that represents the difference between the purchase price of a business, or of selected assets and liabilities of that business, and book value.

gross margin   A measure of profitability, equal to revenue minus cost of goods sold divided by revenue. (The term is sometimes used for only the dollar amount of revenue minus cost of goods sold, although the latter is more often called gross profit.)

gross profit   See *gross margin*.

income statement   See *profit and loss statement*.

indirect cost   Cost not directly related or assignable to the production of specific revenue, products, or services.

"indirect of direct" cost   Indirect cost incurred by people who normally charge their time to direct cost; e.g., training time for assembly workers.

intangible asset   A nonphysical thing that will have value over an appreciable period of time, such as a patent or trademark.

inventory   The physical material and products that a business owns for future production of revenue.

liability   Something of value owned by a business, i.e., a valid claim that someone holds on assets of the business.

long-term debt   A debt that is not due for payment for more than one year.

long-term liability   Any liability that represents an obligation that need not be discharged within one year.

margin   A measure of profitability that is a ratio of revenue minus selected costs to revenue. (Also sometimes used as the dollar amount of revenue minus selected costs.) See *contribution margin; gross margin;* and *profit margin*.

markup   A measure of profitability equal to revenue minus cost (typically, direct cost or purchase cost) divided by that same cost. (The term is sometimes used for the dollar amount of revenue minus cost.)

net asset value   See *equity*.

Glossary of Accounting Terms Used in Budgeting

net income Revenue minus all expense for an accounting period, including federal and foreign income tax. In common usage, the same as profit after tax.

"net of _____" After the item represented by the blank is subtracted out; e.g., "profit net of income taxes" is profit after tax.

net worth See *equity*.

operating statement See *profit and loss statement*.

orders received Binding agreements by customers to buy products or services for future delivery.

overhead Indirect cost. More often used to describe indirect cost in a particular function or activity closely associated with production of revenue but not assignable to a particular product or service. Typical classes of overhead are manufacturing labor overhead, manufacturing material overhead, engineering overhead, and service overhead.

overhead pool A cost pool for a particular type of overhead.

overhead rate The percentage rate at which a particular overhead cost is added to particular direct cost, calculated by dividing the applicable overhead cost by total direct cost.

percentage of completion A method of accounting, used for large and long contracts, that recognizes revenue during the course of the contract in accordance with the proportion of work that has been completed or with cost that has been incurred.

period cost Cost expensed during the same period in which it is incurred.

prepaid expense An asset representing an amount paid for purchases not yet received, i.e., a right to those purchases in the future.

prepaid revenue A liability representing payment received for future products or services, i.e., an obligation to supply those products or services in the future.

present value The equivalent value today of a future receipt or disbursement, with a specified interest rate.

profit Revenue minus expense, the financial gain of a business.

profit after tax Revenue minus all expense. The same as net income.

profit and loss statement (P&L) The financial statement that presents all revenue and expense and resulting profit or loss, by conventional categories, of a company for a time period. It is also called the income statement and the operating statement.

profit before tax Profit before accounting for federal and foreign income tax expense.

profit center An organizational unit for which revenue, expense, and profit are budgeted and accumulated, and which is responsible for profit.

profit margin A performance measure equal to revenue minus total expense divided by revenue.

raw materials inventory The portion of inventory that consists of purchased material that will be used to make revenue-producing products, and the value of that material.

receipt An amount of cash received.

residual value The salvage or scrap value remaining at the end of the life of a tangible asset.

retained earnings The accumulated amount of profit retained by a business, i.e., not paid out to shareholders.

return on assets (ROA) Profit divided by assets, a measure of the percentage of the value of its assets that is earned by a business.

return on capital (ROC) Profit divided by capital, a measure of the percentage of total investment earned by a business.

return on equity (ROE) Profit divided by equity, a measure of the percentage of the owners' investment earned by a business.

return on investment (ROI) For an entire business, synonymous with return on capital. For a given capital investment within a business, the ratio of the profit that will result to the amount of the investment.

revenue The amount of past, current, and future receipts that are earned and recorded in a given period, in accordance with Generally Accepted Accounting Principles.

sales Generally used interchangeably with revenue but sometimes restricted to only the revenue that results from the purchase of products by customers (as opposed to, e.g., service revenue).

schedule A written, numerical presentation of particular accounting information, such as an inventory schedule or an indirect cost schedule.

short-term debt Debt that must be paid within a year.

short-term liability A liability that must be discharged within a year.

standard cost A calculated, anticipated cost of a product under given conditions that will be used as expense when sale of that product is recorded on the P&L.

stockholders' equity Strictly speaking, the equity of a corporation, as opposed to a partnership or a proprietorship. Ordinarily used synonymously with equity, net worth, and net asset value.

tangible asset A physical asset.

transfer price The price charged by one element of a company for products or services supplied to another element of the same company.

turnover The rate at which an asset is used and replaced, most often applied to inventory. It is expressed as the ratio of a year's revenue to the amount of the asset. Inventory turnover is the reciprocal, in different terms, of days inventory. (In British accounting, "turnover" is the term used for what Americans call "revenue.")

variable cost   Cost that varies with revenue.

variance   The amount by which an actual financial parameter, such as a cost, differs from its standard or budgeted value.

working capital   Current assets minus current liabilities.

work in progress inventory   The portion of inventory that consists of partially completed products and the associated burdened labor and material costs.

Appendix C
Use of Personal Computers in Budgeting

The purpose of this appendix is to provide useful information on the application of personal computers to a manager's budgeting work. The subject is not budgeting software, i.e., the programs that the company uses to put together its various budgets. Budgeting software is the province of accounting and top management. Nor is the subject use of personal computers in general; that is beyond our scope.

Through personal or desktop computers, computer power is economically accessible to nearly everyone in business. You do not have to be a computer expert to obtain good value from personal computers. Applications that can help you in budgeting, as well as management in general, are not difficult to learn.

Personal Computer Hardware and Software

There are numerous combinations of computer hardware and software available for the desktop. There are two general families of personal computers, IBM and Apple. The former are more commonly used in business. IBM and IBM-compatibles have a wealth of software available for them—operating systems, graphics, databases, and almost any application imaginable.

If you are choosing your own desktop computing system, the correct sequence is to begin with what you want to do, your application(s). First choose the available software that best meets your needs, then the printer, and last the computer that adequately handles the chosen software and printer.

The more typical company situation is that management information systems (MIS) has chosen standard hardware and software for use by everyone. The only decision you have to make is the way you wish to use the computer; appropriate standard hardware and software is then supplied to you.

If you have specialized needs to compute something frequently, there is probably a specialized software package available to do it. MIS or you can find the package. However, in general, you can do most of the computations applicable to budgeting on a spreadsheet program. There are three leading spreadsheet programs on the market: Lotus 1-2-3 by Lotus Development, Excel by Microsoft, and Quattro Pro by Borland International. Lotus 1-2-3 was first on the scene and has the biggest user base, but each has its champions.

Spreadsheet Programs

A spreadsheet program displays numbers in a column-row format and provides the means to mathematically or logically relate entries in particular positions (or "cells") to other entries in the spreadsheet. Thus it allows you to provide a wide variety and large quantity of data input and calculations to get numerical results.

A simple example is the calculation of monthly sales by region. The spreadsheet can be designed so that columns are months and rows are the different regions. When data are received on regional monthly sales, they are entered in the appropriate cell. The spreadsheet is programmed to add all the rows in a given column to give total sales for the month and can also be programmed to add across the rows, giving a running total of sales by each region across the year as well as a year-to-date value for total sales. This much could be done easily by hand. However, if you want to see totals by region, by product, and by salesperson, for a large number of each, the spreadsheet can be programmed to present totals in all the different ways you want to see them. If data are entered correctly, they are inputted only once and all the various desired results are immediately available.

Thus one use of a spreadsheet is large-scale manipulation of data, with the added advantage that the potential for arithmetic errors in large-volume calculations is avoided. More valuable is its use in planning. Whatever the subject, a spreadsheet allows "what if" analysis to be done for the ranges of conditions (inputs) you choose to examine.

Results of changing an input parameter can be viewed, graphed, or numerically printed with little effort.

There are many examples of things that can be done this way and yield useful information to managers. Purchasing managers can track all purchase orders, with the ability to sort them by size and by the originating organization. Engineering and factory planning managers can capture the source and costs of engineering change notices, for later analysis of the process and the trends and payoffs of change notices by product. For a sales force, tracking sales calls, expense, and orders by customer and by salesperson allows a variety of sales analyses to be done and commissions to be computed.

What has been done in all these cases is to gather data for a model of part of an organization's work—activities, inputs, and outputs—on the computer as an aid in planning the work. Modeling is the most fruitful application of personal computers to a manager's budgeting tasks. Before discussing it at greater length, however, we will cover two other useful applications of personal computers to budgeting.

Computerized Budget Forms

ENLIGHTENED, INC., supplies managers with personal computer diskettes rather than paper budget forms. MUDDLED, INC., uses paper budget forms.

If you receive paper budget forms, the first worthwhile personal computer application to budgeting is to program the forms onto a spreadsheet on your personal computer. As the budgeting process proceeds, your budget forms will undoubtedly have to be revised a number of times. Having the forms on the spreadsheet minimizes the work involved in revision, as well as facilitates analysis of alternatives, accuracy and consistency, and a record of changes and reasoning (discussed in the next section).

In programming any spreadsheet it is important to design the spreadsheet so that inputs flow automatically to wherever they are used. This minimizes later data entry work; more important, it eliminates a major source of error and inconsistency. For example, an overhead rate may be used five times in your budget form. It should be manually inputted only once and transferred to all the places used by computer instruction internal to the spreadsheet program. The alternative of five different manual inputs almost ensures error and inconsistency; at some revision in the process, you will forget to make one or more entries of a revised overhead rate. This requirement is obvious to technically trained people, but experience has shown that it is not obvious to all people who design spreadsheets. (Even technically trained people will sometimes not properly interconnect a new module or other addition to an existing spreadsheet.) Similarly, numbers calculated in the spreadsheet should never be brought out for later manual input; they should flow automatically in the computer to wherever they are needed.

Keeping a Record of Reasoning and Changes

The "Tips and Traps" section at the end of Chapter 13 exhorted managers to keep careful notes of the assumptions, reasoning, and calculations behind each budget submission and modification. The reason is the anticipated changes resulting from all the level-by-level budget reviews, and the possibility that, weeks later, managers may not otherwise remember the basis of a particular number when it is attacked.

This can be done by hand, retaining all working papers and making notes on them as the work is done. It is easier if budget forms and the models used for calculations are on a personal computer. Spreadsheets include the capability to add textual notes and explanations, and are dated. Calculations for a particular set of input values and the form for a particular budget revision should be saved. They can be saved on the computer disk or diskette or on paper, or both, according to personal preference.

An engineering manager can put her manpower planning on a spreadsheet, as discussed in Chapter 9. She may also have programmed other simple models she finds useful, such as an overhead rate model and perhaps a project quoting model. If she does these before budgeting begins, she has a head start in her planning and can react quickly and possibly influence the output requirements she is given for her budget. At that time, she should also put her budget forms on a spreadsheet. If her budget goes through three revisions, the result will be four versions of the budget forms. She will also have a large number of manpower planning layouts and other model analyses. These will include preliminary, prebudget planning and probably one or two alternatives that she has studied in addition to those submitted. She should save all of these until the budget receives final approval. Further, she should save what she believes are the most important or probable alternatives through most of next year, as an aid in reacting to the changes and surprises that will surely appear.

Modeling

Mathematical models are equations or sets of equations that express mathematical relationships among parameters. Modeling can be extremely complex and sophisticated. Models used in weather forecasting are so complex that meaningful analysis was not practical until the advent of supercomputers. Simulations that predict performance based on mathematical expressions of physical relationships have long been used in the design of aircraft, missiles, automobiles, turbines, and many other complex machines. Each such use of modeling involves a professional specialty and extensive research and literature.

The Nature of Business Models

Fortunately, the models useful in budgeting are not complex mathematically; they require only simple algebra and arithmetic. The summary equations that describe the financial status and results of a business are, after all, simple equations:

$$\text{Equity} = \text{Assets} - \text{Liabilities}$$
$$\text{Profit} = \text{Revenue} - \text{Expense}$$
$$\text{Cash Flow} = \text{Receipts} - \text{Disbursements}$$

Business models are expansions and manipulations of these three basic equations or, in the case of a functional organization, equations that relate costs and outputs to activities and inputs.

While practical business models contain many terms, a simple expansion of the profit equation yields a model that is useful in analyzing the break-even point of a company. In the above profit equation, if expense E is expanded into variable expense E_v and fixed expense E_f, the above equation becomes the following (P stands for profit, R for revenue):

$$P = R - (E_v + E_f)$$

Since contribution margin m can be expressed as

$$m = (R - E_v) / R$$

then

$$mR = R - E_v$$

and, substituting mR for R − E_v, the equation for profit can be written as

$$P = mR - E_f$$

That is, profit equals contribution margin times revenue minus fixed expense. Setting profit to zero, the revenue at which the business will break even for given values of contribution margin and fixed expense is

$$R = E_f / m$$

Thus, if margin is 40 percent, the revenue needed to break even is 2.5 times the fixed expense.

An example of a functional organization cost model was given in Chapter 9 for a machine shop, wherein the cost incurred on one machine was

Machine Cost = Labor Rate × (Setup Time + Operating Time) + Material per Unit × Number of Units + Electrical Rate × Time per Unit × Number of Units

Summing this cost for each machine yields total machining costs, and thus the total cost of the machine shop, for a given quantity and mix of output:

Total Cost = Sum of Each Machine Cost + Overhead

Another useful type of business model does not use equations specifically. Rather, it "spreads" pertinent parameters in a table versus time. The engineering manpower model referred to above is of this type. Cash flow is often modeled this way—columns of the spreadsheet are months, while rows are various categories of expected receipts and disbursements. The spreadsheet then sums all receipts and all disbursements for the month, and the difference between total receipts and disbursements is cash flow for the month.

As a simple example of such a cash flow model, consider a project to build and ship $1,000 of a particular product, $200 per month in the third through seventh months of the project. Material costs are expected to be 40 percent of revenue (i.e., $80 for each month's shipments), and material must be received one month before shipment. Materials will be paid for one month after receipt. Labor and other project costs have been estimated at 30 percent of sales during each shipment month (i.e., $60 in months three through seven). Payments are expected from the customer two months after shipment. A cash flow model of this project is shown in Figure C-1. This simple model shows the maximum investment (negative $280 cumulative cash flow in the fourth month), the time at which the investment is recovered (cumulative cash flow becomes positive in the eighth month), and total cash flow from the project ($300). This type of model is often the best way to show timing relationships.

The complexities in business models do not come from the mathematics. They come from the number of terms that make up each element of the simple equations. Companies have many types of costs and usually many products. Organizations have many types of activities and expense, and usually a number of outputs. Profit or margin is usually desired by product or business line or division.

With current personal computers and spreadsheets, there is no reason not to expand business models as far as necessary to achieve the necessary degree of realism. A business might have fifty types of product and price combinations, with different kinds and quantities of expense associated with each. This kind of complexity makes manual analysis difficult but poses no problem for a computer spreadsheet.

Figure C-1. Project cash flow model.

	Months									Total
	1	2	3	4	5	6	7	8	9	
Material received		$ 80	$ 80	$ 80	$ 80	$ 80				$ 400
Material paid			80	80	80	80	$ 80			400
Labor/other expense			60	60	60	60	60			300
Shipments (revenue)			200	200	200	200	200			1,000
Receipts					200	200	200	200	200	1,000
Cash flow*	0	0	−140	−140	60	60	60	200	200	300
Cumulative cash flow	0	0	−140	−280	−220	−160	−100	100	300	

*Cash flow = Receipts − Materials paid − Labor − Other expenses

Use of Modeling by Managers

The models that are useful to managers in budgeting are those that relate the elements of the definition of the organization's work—activities, outputs, inputs, output dictators, and cost drivers. As discussed in Chapter 9, models must be used when no valid data or trends exist for a budget number that must be generated. They should be used as a supplement and reasonableness check for data and trends. And they can be used in a variety of cases as a powerful aid to the planning work of budgeting. The results needed from the organization models are always costs and usually outputs.

Every organization has its own models because each has unique activity-output-input relationships. Some are straightforward, some are elusive. The previous machine shop example was extensive, with an equation for each machine and many terms in each equation. However, it was straightforward, because the activity-output-input relationships are straightforward. On the other hand, some staff organizations have an almost constant cost level regardless of changes in outputs. A payroll function may serve 3,000 employees, and discover that it needs the same number of payroll clerks to serve 2,000 or 4,000. (Knowing that there is an irreducible "kernel" of payroll cost for a given set of procedures and processes is useful information, of course. Thus the analysis that determined same was useful, even if a crisp relationship did not result.)

The key to development of useful models is the identification of output dictators and cost drivers in the definition of the organization's work (Chapters 5 and 6). Building the model then consists of expressing, either in equation form or in the time-spread form, the relationships identified in that definition of work.

Each organization's models are unique, but we can give some examples:

- In the machine shop example (Chapters 6 and 9 and above), the cost model relates machine shop cost to the use of the different machines. The production schedule, a principal cost determinant, is the dictator of how much each machine is used. The level of automation and procedures and processes is implicit in the model—i.e., new machines or different processes would require different equations.

- A common problem is to satisfy maximum waiting-time requirements for customers in a transaction situation, such as in a restaurant, in teller operations in a bank, or in switching of telephone calls.

Rigorous treatment of complex waiting time/peaking situations requires sophisticated application of queuing theory. However, managers can handle many normal business situations to a satisfactory approximation with simple arithmetic and algebra. As a simple example, consider a teller transaction in a bank that averages five minutes and a service standard that is to keep no customer waiting more than ten minutes on the average. In this case, seven tellers are required to handle a peak of twenty-one customers entering the bank at the same time. (For n tellers, average transaction time T, and N customers arriving simultaneously, the equation for the longest average waiting time W is

$$W = (NT / n) - T$$

Solving for n,

$$n = NT / (W + T)$$

If n is not exactly a whole number, the next highest whole number is the practical answer.)

- A recruiting manager's definition of work yields the expected conclusion that his strongest cost driver is simply the number of positions to be filled, or new hires. His model is simply

$$\text{Cost} = \text{Constant} + (\text{Another Constant}) \times (\text{New Hires})$$

Analysis of current and past data and trends yields good approximations for the two constants. There are two sources of required new hires: expansion in the division he serves, and turnover. In such a service organization, the manager must wait for next year's plans for the entire division before he knows the personnel expansion number to use. He must estimate turnover from data and trends, questioned and analyzed for changing conditions. (The recruiting manager's budget should clearly include two assumptions [see Chapter 7]: division personnel increases and turnover rates. This is a prime example of an organization's costs being determined by factors beyond the manager's control.)

Remember that models are always approximations of reality. Models are used in budgeting not because they are completely accurate. They are used because they are more accurate than any other source of numbers in an uncertain world. Further, in that uncertain world there is no benefit in introducing complexity just to get answers precise to three decimal places. Certainty about next year is impossible in any case; models react to uncertainty better than invalid data or trends because they have a logical basis and provide an immediate rationale to deal with changes and surprises.

Getting Started With Modeling

Approaching the subject for the first time, managers probably do not now the specific analyses and models they want. In such a case, they should first decide the data they believe will be useful. Then they can design spreadsheets for data capture that can be sorted in various ways. As familiarity increases, various analyses of that data will suggest themselves. This leads to additions of models (equations) to the spreadsheet.

The spreadsheet readily holds large amounts and varieties of data, much more than is practical in a manual system. The difficulty is in initially knowing which data will be wanted later. The suggestion is to start by capturing all data of conceivable interest, but you have to promise to weed some out as relative importance becomes better known. Otherwise, the data generation becomes an onerous end in itself.

The recommended sequence is to start with two things in parallel. Think about what costs, activities, inputs, and outputs should be captured. At the same time, investigate what programs and information are already available. The company information system might already supply the needed information, or something close to it. People in MIS, accounting, or other managers may already have spreadsheet programs that will meet your needs. The ideal is to use the company system if possible. The next best thing is to download data from the company system to a personal computer for analysis by a program already developed. Do not duplicate things already available. However, if this investigation yields no results, the task is then to design and program the desired model spreadsheets, or have someone do it for you.

As with everything else, results improve with effort and time. Personal computers can be frustrating and contrary beasts to first-time users. If you read the reference manuals and get help from MIS, you will soon be computing with facility and wondering how you ever got along without your personal computer.

Bibliography

This bibliography presents sources of information on major topics closely related to budgeting.

Accounting

The suggested sources of accounting knowledge for managers are basic accounting textbooks, books written to explain accounting to nonaccountants, and accounting handbooks. A representative list of these is presented below. Included is a book on a special topic—activity-based accounting—because this is a new technique that can facilitate the processes of budgeting and management.

Brimson, James A. *Activity Accounting.* New York: McGraw-Hill, 1991.

Griffin, Michael P. *Intermediate Finance and Accounting for Nonfinancial Managers.* New York: AMACOM, 1991.

Margolis, Neal, and Harmon, N. Paul. *Accounting Essentials.* New York: Wiley, 1991.

Needles, Belverd E., Jr.; Anderson, Henry R.; and Caldwell, James C. *Principles of Accounting.* Boston: Houghton Mifflin, 1984.

Siegel, Joel G., and Shim, Jae K. *Barron's Accounting Handbook.* New York: Barron's, 1990.

Also, the American Management Association periodically presents a popular three-day seminar entitled "Fundamentals of Finance and Accounting for Nonfinancial Executives." For information, contact American Management Association, P.O. Box 319, Saranac Lake, NY 12983-9988. The telephone number is (518) 891-0065.

Capital Budgeting

Books on the subject of capital budgeting are scarce. However, relevant information is contained in various accounting manuals; the best source for these are the accounting professionals in your company. Capital budgeting is also treated in portions of books on financial management. Two representative books on that subject, with the location of the capital budgeting coverage indicated, are as follows:

> Brigham, Eugene F. *Fundamentals of Financial Management* (Part III). Chicago: The Dryden Press, 1989.
>
> Pappas, James L.; Brigham, Eugene F.; and Hirschey, Mark. *Managerial Economics* (Chapter 13). Chicago: The Dryden Press, 1983.

In addition, Siegel and Shim, *Barron's Accounting Handbook*, cited in the section above, covers various ways to evaluate capital investments on pages 171 to 181.

Compensation Planning

Compensation is a popular subject, but articles and books tend to be advanced or specialized. Comprehensive introductions to the subject are the following:

> McCoy, Thomas J. *Compensation and Motivation*. New York: AMACOM, 1992.
>
> Patten, Thomas H., Jr. *PAY: Employee Compensation and Incentive Plans*. New York: The Free Press, 1979.
>
> Rock, Milton L. *Compensation Handbook*, 3d ed. New York: McGraw-Hill, 1991.
>
> Sibson, Robert E. *Compensation*, 5th ed. New York: AMACOM, 1990.

Management and Planning

There are many, many management and planning books. The following are listed because they cover, with different emphases, aspects of management and planning that are closely related to budgeting:

> Donnelly, Robert M. *Guidebook to Planning*. New York: AMACOM, 1984.
>
> Finney, Robert G. *Powerful Budgeting for Better Planning and Management*. New York: AMACOM, 1993.
>
> Kami, Michael. *Trigger Points*. New York: McGraw-Hill, 1988.
>
> Porter, Michael E. *Competitive Advantage*. New York: The Free Press, 1985.
>
> Thomsett, Michael. *Winning Numbers*. New York: AMACOM, 1990.

No management bibliography is complete without books by Peter Drucker, all of which are recommended. His most comprehensive treatment of management is *Management: Tasks, Responsibilities, Practices.* New York: Harper & Row, 1973.

Use of Personal Computers

There are shelves and shelves of books about the use of personal computers in any bookstore. There are books on personal computers in general, books on particular personal computers, and books on particular applications. The more popular software packages all have a number of books written solely about them. There are also numerous seminars on general computing subjects and on particular computers, applications, and software packages.

The best sources of information about personal computers are usually the experts in management information systems (MIS) in your company. MIS people are also the best people for advice on books and seminars about the particular computers and software you wish to learn to use.

Here is a list of general books on personal computing, spreadsheets, and Lotus 1-2-3 (the most popular spreadsheet program):

Altman. Rebecca, et al. *Using 1-2-3, Release 3.1,* 2d ed. Carmel, Ind.: Que Corporation, 1990.

Capron, H. L., and Perron, John D. *Computers & Information Systems: Tools for an Information Age.* Redwood City, Calif.: Benjamin/Cummings Publishing, 1993.

Desposito, Joseph, et al. *Using 1-2-3, Release 2.3,* special ed. Carmel, Ind.: Que Corporation, 1991.

Murray, Katherine. *Introduction to Personal Computers.* Carmel, Ind.: Que Corporation, 1990.

Thommes, M. C. *Proper Spreadsheet Design.* Boston: Boyd & Fraser Publishing, 1992.

Thomsett, Rob. *Third Wave Project Management.* Englewood Cliffs, N.J.: Prentice Hall, 1993.

Index

accounting, 56
  in budgeting, 159–171
  terms of, 173–179
accrual accounting, 122, 161
action planning, 33
action program, 79–80, 82, 86
actions, 32
activities, 34, 41, 46–48, 53, 63, 65
activity statements, 46–47
added capacity, 130–131
advertising costs, 58
allocated costs, 166–167
amortization, 126, 164
approval, 151–158
assembly units, 13
assets, 161–162
assumptions, 13, 33, 35, 41, 42, 67–76, 92, 153
  order and revenue, 103–104
automation, 61, 74

back orders, 60
backlog, 105
backward reasoning, 33–34
balance sheet, 161–162
benefits expense, 57
bought costs, 56, 57–58
budget, 1–2, 17–18
  annual, 18–19
  approval of, 6, 151–158

communication of, 6–7
company, 10–11
in control and measurement, 18
importance of, 19–20
information in, 11–13
manager's, 11–13
numbers generation in, 6, 147–148
padding of, 76
preliminary, 146–147
preliminary targets of, 15
proper content of, 91–99
reasons for, 18–19
review of, 9, 17–18, 149
budget analysts, 17
budget forms, 13–17, 20, 183–184
budgetary quotation, 116
budgeting, 1–2, 24–25
  complexity of, 9–10
  computers used in, 181–190
  gap analysis in, 81–83
  goal of, 39
  inherent problems of, 22
  iterations of, 42–43
  nature of, 5–27
  planning work of, 31–87
  preparatory work for, 144–146
  process of, 16–18, 141–149
  scope of, for managers, 5–7
  what to expect in, 9–20
  work of, 141–144

burden rates, 167–168, 170
business models, 185–187
business plan, 36–38

calendar year, 19
capacity, revenue and, 102
capital, 58, 137
   budgeting of, 125–137
capital budget, 15, 125–126, 134–137
capital expenditure, 125, 132, 164
   categories of, 127–131
capital forecast, 6
capital requests, 126
cash, 14
cash accounting, 161
cash flow, 14, 160–161
   discounted, 129
   modeling of, 186–187
communication, 6–7, 80–81, 86, 148
   in approval process, 155
company budget, 10–11
compensation planning, 118–119
competition, 50, 102
computers
   budget forms for, 183–184
   in budgeting, 181–190
   hardware and software of, 181–182
   modeling with, 185–190
   spreadsheet programs for, 182–183
consolidation process, 17–18
contingency plans, 33, 35
contracts, long-term, 109
contribution margin, 171, 185–186
control, 18
corporate allocation, 13–14
cost burdens, 167
cost drivers, 41, 45, 59–65, 73
cost entries, timing of, 121–123
cost estimating, 114–115, 121–123
   for new activities, 120–121
   of personnel costs, 117–118
   of purchase costs, 116
   for salary planning, 118–119
cost model, 96–97
cost reserves, 122

cost trends, 95
costs, 12, 55, 56–58, 63–64
   calculation of, 74, 185–186
   estimation of, 113–123
   in organization's work, 62–65
   in planning, 34–35
   prediction of, 9
   reduction of, 59, 129–130
   relationships of, 58–59, 64
   standard, 169
   total, 13
costs forecast, 6
credibility, 22, 158
customer demands, 50
cycles, predictive, 18–19

data, 92
   direct, 91–94, 98–99, 105, 107–108, 114, 148
   stretching of, 93–94
depreciation, 126, 164
direct expense, 164–165
disbursements, 14, 160

economy, relevant, 102
employees, costs of, 118
environmental factors, 154–156
   internal, 155
equipment replacement, 127
equity, 162
errors, 153
expected status quo result, 78–79
expense, 13, 126–127, 163–165
   indirect, 165
   treatments of, 165–166

facilities-related costs, 58
factory assembly, 12–13
financial analysts, 34–35, 115
financial measures, 169–171
financial results, 10, 19, 23–24
financial statements, 39, 159
fiscal year, 19
flow chart, 52
forecasting
   of major orders, 108–109

Index

of prices, 104–105
revenue, 101–111
forms, 13–15, 16–17, 20
fringe benefits, 13
future, uncertainty of, 6, 24, 36–37, 41, 54, 67–76

gap analysis, 6, 42, 77–86, 145, 152
   advantages and benefits of, 86–87
   division profit, 79–80
   interorganization, 86
gap dimension, 78, 81–84
general and administrative expense, 166–167
Generally Accepted Accounting Principles (GAAP), 165
goals, 32, 33, 78–79, 80–82
   budgeting, 39
   of gap analysis, 83
   ultimate vs. working, 40
goods sold, cost of, 15
government regulations, 49–50
gross margin, 15, 170–171

implementation, 44
information, 11–13, 34, 115
   excessive, 44
   negative, 87
   outputs of, 48, 63
   supplemental, 12–13
input accounting, 168–169
inputs, 41, 46–48, 51–53, 63, 115
instructions, 51
   distribution of, 16–17
interim accomplishments, 33
internal environmental factors, 154–155
internal uncontrollable factors (IUF), 68–69, 71–74, 76, 145
interorganizational problems, 54
inventory, 58, 164, 165–166, 168
inventory schedule, 15
investment costs, 58

Kami, Michael, on gap analysis, 78n

labor
   costs of, 15, 56–57, 59, 97
   direct, 56–57, 165, 168–169
   indirect, 56–57
legal requirements, 49
level of effort functions, 50
liabilities, 58, 162

machinery, 74
   cost of new, 65
machining costs, 96
make costs, 56–57
management, 1
   measurement of, 68
manager
   budget of, 11–13, 17
   in budgeting process, 141–149
   modeling used by, 188–190
   objectives of, 22–23
   prebudgeting activity of, 15–16
   scope of budgeting for, 5–7
manufacturing
   bought costs in, 57
   special problems of, 168–169
manufacturing vice-president's budget, 14–15
margins, 170–171, 185–186
market, 49, 102
marketing effort, 102
material flow, 47
materials, 51
measurement
   budget for, 18
   fair, 87
   of management, 23–24
method, 32
milestones, 33, 35
model-type thinking, 93–94
models, 91–92, 95–99, 108, 145, 148, 185–190
   in cost budgeting, 114–115
   pricing, 105
   for revenue budgeting, 106–107

new activities budgeting, 120–121
new capability, 130–131

new products cost, 131
numbers
    in capital budget, 135–137
    in cost estimation, 113–123
    generation of, 91–137, 143–144
    justifications of, 152–153
    revenue, 106–108
    sources of, 91–99
numerical forecasts, 6

objectives, conflict of, 21–23
operations, 47
order cycle, 108
orders, 105
    assumptions about, 103–104
    forecasting of, 108–110
organization work flow, 40–41, 52–54
organization's work, 40–41, 45–54, 145, 146
    in assumptions process, 70–71
    costs of, 62–65
    flow of, 40–41, 52–54
    planning of, 5–6, 62–65
    value and validity of, 152
output accounting, 168–169
output dictators, 41, 45, 49–51, 63, 73
outputs, 41–42, 46–48, 53, 61, 65
    in planning, 53, 62–63
    prediction of, 12
    primary, 48, 62
    required, 60, 64
    resulting vs. required, 43
outside environmental factors (OEF), 67–69, 71–74, 76, 102–103, 145
outside factors, uncontrollability of, 24–25, 41
outside requirements, 49–50
    driver of, 60
outside services
    costs of, 58
    increased use of, 59
overhead expense, 96, 166, 167–168
overhead schedule, 15
overtime costs, 59
owner, objectives of, 22

padding, 137, 157
payback period analysis, 129
payroll budget form, 13–14, 14
performance improvement, 6, 41–42, 64–65, 143
    cost drivers and, 60
    gap analysis in, 77–87
    nonquantifiable, 128–129
personal characteristics, 153
personnel costs, 58, 117–118
plan
    defense and justification of, 33, 35
    predicting financial results of, 9
planning, 5–6, 39–43, 143
    bad, 38–39
    of budget costs, 114
    in budgeting, 31–87, 142–143
    compensation, 118–119
    gap analysis and, 84–86
    implementation and, 44
    inherent problems of, 27
prebudgeting activity, 15–16
predicted results, 82–83
president, objectives of, 22
price
    forecasting of, 104–105
    level of, 61
problems, 54
procedures, 61
processes, 47, 61
product/service maturity, 102
production plan, 74
professionals, cost of, 59
profit before tax, 14
profit margin, 171
profit and loss (P&L) budget, 13–14, 162–166
project cash flow model, 186–187
project companies, special problems of, 168–169
promotion costs, 58
psychological factors, 156–157
psychological games, 70
purchase costs, 116

receipts, 14, 160
regulatory requirements, 49–50
reorganization, 53, 54
resources, 33–35, 47
responsibility assignment, 37
results-oriented activity, 34
return on assets (ROA), 170
return on capital (ROC), 169–170
return on equity (ROE), 169–170
return on investment (ROI), 127, 170
 calculations of, 131–134
revenue, 15, 39–40, 60, 103–104, 162–163
 averaging of, 110
 derivatives of, 49, 60
 forecasting of, 101–111
 numbers in, 106–108
revenue budgeting, 105–106, 111
 quarterly, 110
 in ranges, 109–110
 special considerations in, 109–110
revenue drivers, 101–103, 106
revenue forecast, 6
revenue trends, 95
reviews, 9, 17, 18, 21, 153

safety/health/regulation requirements, 127–128
salaries, 56–57, 164–165
 budgeting of, 118
 planning of, 118–119
sales, 13, 60, 102
sales backlog, 91
sales department budget, 11
sales relationships, derivative, 110
schedule, 33
scheduling, 43, 145–146
 backward, 34
seasonal trends, 94–95, 122–123
seasonal variation, 109
service, definition of, 34
service outputs, 48, 63

service requests, 50, 60
severance costs, 122
specificity, 37
spreadsheet, 98
 programs for, 182–183
status quo result, 82
stock, 58
structural factors, 50, 60
supplemental information, 12–13
suppliers, 74
support costs, 58

task force, 86
tasks, 47
tools, 51
top management, prebudgeting activity of, 15
trends, 91–92, 98–99, 114, 148
 direct data and, 108
 misuse of, 95
 price, 104–105
 revenue, 107
 seasonal, 94–95, 122–123

uncertainty, 6, 24, 36–37, 41, 54, 67–76
uncontrollable factors, 24–26, 41
 identification of, 145
 internal, 71–76
 in revenue, 102–103
units assembled summaries, 15
unusual expenses, 122

variances, 169

wage costs, 57
wages, 118, 164–165
work
 costs of, 117
 definition of, 52–54
 of new organization, 53
 see also labor; organization's work